NORWICH
in the
AMERICAN REVOLUTION

NORWICH
in the
AMERICAN REVOLUTION

PATRICIA F. STALEY

Published by The History Press
An imprint of Arcadia Publishing
Charleston, SC
www.historypress.com

First published 2025

Manufactured in the United States

ISBN 9781467159968

Library of Congress Control Number: 2025943423

For Juliana,
the youngest Staley

and

For the men and women of colonial Norwich
who risked everything to create a new nation.

CONTENTS

PREFACE

This book began as a walking tour of the Norwichtown Green that I was preparing for the Leffingwell House Museum. As I researched, I learned that Benedict Arnold's wasn't the only Revolutionary War story from Norwich. There were plenty of other people who endured hardships and fear, people who lost fortunes by supporting the cause, who accepted they would be hanged if the Americans failed to win the war.

What we now call Norwichtown *was* Norwich for the town's first century. The people who lived around the Green and in the surrounding area were the patriots who helped create a nation. Some were wealthy and prominent and entertained George Washington and Governor Jonathan Trumbull. Others, the "ordinary folks," watched from the side of the road as General Washington and his troops rode through town. Each of them has a story that should be told, and those stories should be preserved.

Frances Manwaring Caulkins's *History of Norwich, Connecticut* is the standard reference for city history prior to the end of the Civil War. She was far more fortunate than modern historians in writing about the Revolutionary War. Caulkins, who was born in 1795, might well have personally known General Jedidiah Huntington or the city's other patriot leaders who lived into the 1800s. When her history was originally published in 1845, people who had known some of the participants in the Revolution were still alive, so she would have had access to firsthand recollections of the war and the Norwich patriots. More recent historians don't have her advantage. There are records, some letters and occasionally a diary or journal, but there isn't enough personal information to create full and detailed profiles of personalities and their thoughts about the events the patriots observed.

Joan Nafie's 1976 book *To the Beat of a Drum* is an excellent study of Norwich during the War for Independence. Also during the 1976 United States Bicentennial, the Connecticut Historical Society published a series of biographies based on the available records, but those, too, had only limited personal information about their subjects.

In the musical *Hamilton*, there's a song called "The Room Where It Happens" which features Aaron Burr as he decides to run for office so he can be one of the decision-makers. Men from Norwich were often in the "room where it happens," as part of Washington's councils of war, in Connecticut's General Assembly and even in the Continental Congress to write the Declaration of Independence and the Articles of Confederation. They were in the thick of things, but it wasn't the Norwich way to seek attention. Norwich men went off—to war, the legislature, wherever they were needed—did their jobs and came home. No fanfare, no accolades, no big deal, even when their contributions were great. Benedict Arnold was the notable exception. He wasn't shy about demanding his due. Neither were other Continental officers, notably Horatio Gates, who were willing to disparage Arnold, whether to further their own careers or for plain spite. Gates was even willing to openly criticize George Washington in hopes he (Gates) would be named commander of the entire Continental army.

I've always thought Norwich was and is a microcosm of the history of the United States. The city's history encompasses all the major eras of the nation's history in the seventeenth, eighteenth and nineteenth centuries. The first settlers arrived in the late 1650s and set the date of the town's founding in June 1659. The town went from being an agricultural community to a commercial and transportation center and then became a manufacturing center. The progression is easily traced in the city's villages: the early settlement at Norwichtown, where colonial homes and buildings still surround the village green; the maritime center at the harbor, once filled with the masts of ships that sailed not only along the Atlantic coast but also to the Caribbean and sometimes Europe; and the central section along Washington Street and Broadway, where the wealthy mill owners of the mid-nineteenth century lived in the Gilded Age mansions that line the streets. In the village of Taftville, thousands of yards of fabric were produced at the huge Ponemah Mill. Company-owned houses that were occupied by the mill hands still stand on streets laid out in a neat grid.

Norwich has a wealth of residences and buildings original to each era in its history, which makes it easier for us in the twenty-first century to walk a bit in the footsteps of those early settlers. Norwich was a microcosm during the Revolution, too. In the mid-1700s, the town was in the forefront of the move to separate from England. Caulkins noted, "No bolder spirit was manifested in Boston than in Norwich." Residents agitated and instituted boycotts; they took the strong actions they deemed necessary to emphasize the strength of their objections. The paradox, of course, is that by demanding their rights as Englishmen, they became citizens of a new nation.

I wrote the chapter on Benedict Arnold during January days when the outside temperature was sixteen degrees Fahrenheit and the wind was blowing at twenty knots or more. When I went outside, I wore a long down coat, boots, tightly knitted mittens and a hat—I was dry but still painfully cold. There was hot food and coffee waiting inside, where the house was reliably warm.

Arnold and his men braved bitter cold, snow and ice, often while soaking wet, as they crossed the Maine woods to Quebec. They went days without adequate food or dry clothes. At Valley Forge, the soldiers endured similar conditions. Many of the men there with General Jedidiah Huntington and Major John Durkee were barely sheltered in huts, with inadequate food and clothing. The Continental army fought in temperatures above one hundred degrees on a June day at Monmouth Courthouse in New Jersey. There was little shade or water, but they persevered. They were the men who left their families for months at a time to fight for independence, whether on the battlefield, in the courtroom or at the statehouse. While not directly exposed to the elements, the delegates who traveled in an unheated coach or carriage—or riding horseback—from Norwich to Hartford, New York or Philadelphia would not have found it a pleasant journey.

Nearly all of them suffered financial losses, regardless of their role in the struggle. If they were away from home, they couldn't run their businesses, so no money was coming in. Soldiers obviously couldn't pursue their trade, but the army wasn't paying them regularly either. Samel Huntington found that his salary didn't cover his expenses as a delegate to the Congress in Philadelphia.

The men of Norwich dropped everything to muster with the militia and march off to protect the coastline when British warships entered Long Island Sound, as Christopher Leffingwell did multiple times during the seven years of war. Their wives were part of the fight as well. It fell to them to find a way to feed and clothe their families while their husbands were away, sometimes for years at a time. They might have had to keep a business going, as Hannah Arnold did for her widowed brother, or perhaps run the farm and tavern, like Martha Durkee.

Yet all these patriots willingly risked, quite literally, "their lives, fortunes and sacred honor" in the cause of Independence. If they failed in their endeavor, their property would be confiscated, and they would almost certainly be hanged as traitors to the Crown. I don't think it's possible to overestimate how much the Revolutionary War patriots endured in the cause of independence. The debt we owe them is huge.

ACKNOWLEDGEMENTS

Norwich, Connecticut, has an extremely vibrant history community. The Revolutionary War people were especially generous in sharing their time, resources and encouragement, which helped make this book possible.

I am especially grateful to Camilla Farlow of the Society of the Leffingwell House Museum/Founders of Norwich for her insights into colonial Norwich, the vignettes she posts on the Leffingwell House Facebook page and her generosity in opening the museum archives to me.

Dayne Rugh, director of Slater Memorial Museum, took time from the last-minute rush that accompanied publication of his own new book to discuss Colonel John Durkee with me. Dayne's book was enormously helpful to me in creating an abbreviated portrait of Durkee; the whole story can be found in *John Durkee: The Forgotten Story of Connecticut's Bold Man from Bean Hill.*

Historian Damien Cregeau also interrupted his own work to consult on this book. He has a special affinity for Jedidiah Huntington, not least because he lives in the general's house, and it will be a treat to read *Portraits of Patriots: Colonel John Trumbull and Five Fellow Patriots from Connecticut in the American Revolution*, his book about Connecticut's generals.

I also owe a debt to Regan Miner, former executive director of the Norwich Historical Society, for all her work to amplify the Norwich story. Thanks to her efforts, the city now has a robust schedule of walking tours, videos and brochures about the historic sites in Norwich. The city's history covers more than three centuries, so there are many.

Others who lent materials, ideas and support include photographer Tom Kaszuba, the late Stacey Moed-Klein and the Reverend Monsignor Anthony Rosaforte. I also want to remember the late William B. (Bill) Stanley for his tireless efforts to give the "Forgotten Founders" like Samuel Huntington the honor they deserve. Bill also deserves credit for reminding us that Benedict Arnold was a hero before he was a traitor. His message went far beyond the borders of Norwich.

As always, the love and support of my husband, Bob, and the rest of our family remain vital to my work. And it's been great fun to watch budding historian Camden as he learns the Norwich story.

CHAPTER 1

MOVING TOWARD SEPARATION

After its founding in 1659, Norwich, Connecticut transitioned from a farming community to a commercial center in fairly short order. Its location was ideal for industry and shipping—halfway between New York and Boston, along two rivers that meet to form a natural harbor from which the Thames River flows into the open waters of Long Island Sound and the Atlantic Ocean.

The city's thirty-nine founders bought the nine-mile-by-nine-mile square that became Norwich and several surrounding towns from the Native Americans known as the Mohegans. The original settlement was largely what is today known as Norwichtown. Each settler was assigned property that included a home lot and land for growing crops. In the early years, they were self-sustaining and used bartering as the main feature of their economy. Before too long, they were growing more crops than they could use and realized the excess could be sold. The harbor about two and a half miles to the south beckoned. Construction of wharves and ships meant trade that opened economic opportunities for many residents.

By 1750, Norwich was a large and prosperous town. With its population of 5,540, Norwich was the largest town in the colony of Connecticut, surpassing New Haven's 5,085 residents. By 1774, the populations of both had increased substantially, and their positions were reversed: New Haven was the largest town, with 8,295 residents, while state records put Norwich's population at 7,327.

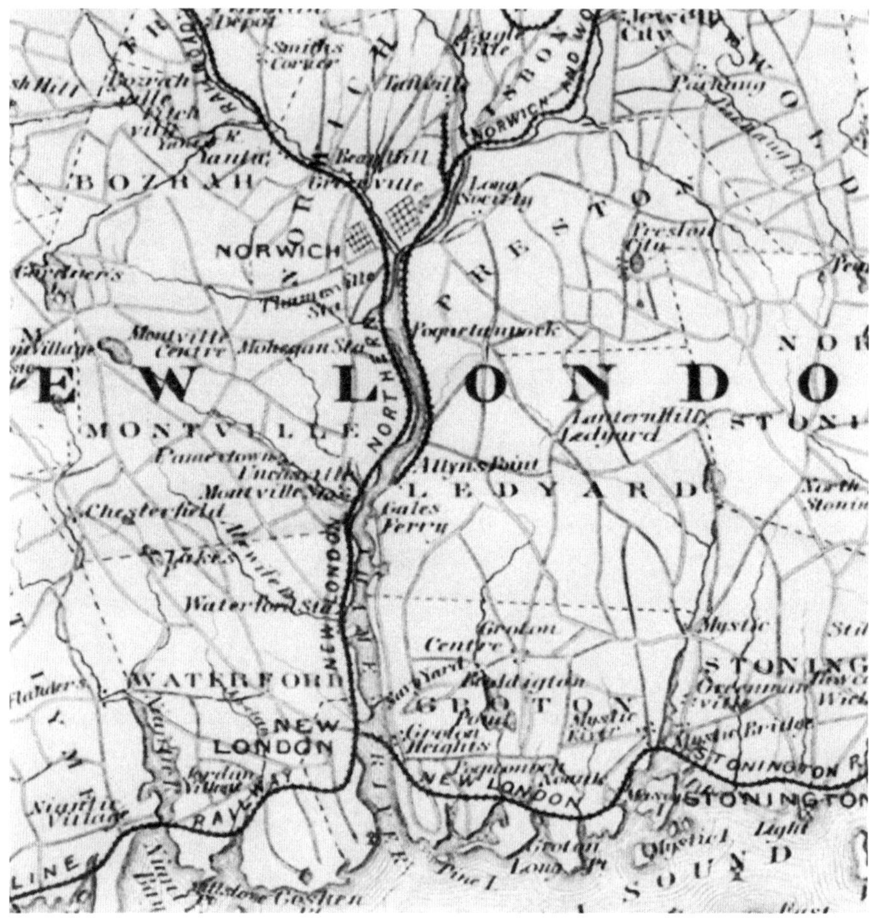

Norwich is at the confluence of the Yantic River (west) and the Shetucket River (east), which forms a natural harbor. From there, the Thames River flows into Long Island Sound. *Courtesy Library of Congress.*

In the mid-eighteenth century, Norwich men, like others in Connecticut, were quite certain they were Englishmen, entitled to the rights and protections every Englishman enjoyed. While other colonies were owned by the king or a board of proprietors, Connecticut was founded under a charter granted by King Charles II, which established a legal basis for self-government in Connecticut. The Connecticut Charter of 1662 explicitly granted the colonists "all liberties and immunities" of the English realm. So seriously did the colonists regard this guarantee of rights that twenty-five years later, they openly defied King James II and New York's royal governor, Sir Edmund Andros. King James wanted to consolidate the northern colonies into a "Dominion of New England" and validate New York's claim that its border reached all the way to the Connecticut River. The new colony would extend from New Jersey to New Hampshire, with Andros as governor. Andros visited each colony in turn to confiscate its charter, declaring it null and void with his appointment.

Accompanied by a group of soldiers, Andros arrived in Hartford in October 1687 and met with the colony's high officials in an upper room at Sanford's tavern. The meeting became the stuff of legend. The charter was lying on a table, leading Andros to expect it would be surrendered. The candles in the room suddenly went dark, naturally leading to some confusion among those in the room. When the candles were lit again, the charter was missing and so was Captain Joseph Wadsworth, who had taken the charter and hidden it in a very large oak tree on Willys Hill in Hartford. The tree, which became known as the Charter Oak, stood until felled by a storm in 1857.

New York's Royal Governor Sir Edmund Andros came to Hartford to revoke Connecticut's colonial charter. *Courtesy Library of Congress.*

Although Andros was forced to leave empty-handed, he ultimately prevailed when the Connecticut General Court declared itself dissolved, leaving Andros in charge. That lasted just over a year, until November 1688, when King James was deposed in favor of King Charles's daughter Mary and her husband, William, and England's Glorious Revolution ended Andros's rule.

In 1689, Connecticut's General Court reinstated the colonial government under all former charters and petitioned Parliament for approval. England's attorney general and solicitor general ruled the charters valid, and the new King William ratified the decisions in April 1694.

For the first half of the eighteenth century, Connecticut prospered as a charter colony with autonomous rule, electing its own governors and making its own laws. Norwich merchants and others grew rich as they developed an active trade along the Eastern Seaboard and in the Caribbean and Europe. The trading pattern that became established was the "triangular trade" of the history books. The Europeans sent ships to Africa to trade or barter European goods, such as copper, cloth, guns and ammunition, for captured Africans, who were taken to Caribbean ports, where sugar plantation owners bought the manufactured goods and the Africans, whom they enslaved. The remaining European goods as well as molasses, sugar and other crops grown on the Caribbean plantations were taken to ports in New England, where molasses and sugar were the main purchases (although some Africans were bought), and in the American South, where plantation owners bought the manufactured goods and Caribbean crops as well as Africans to work in their cotton and tobacco fields. The molasses was distilled into rum, which was shipped to Europe, along with lumber and animal pelts from the North and tobacco, cotton and rice from Southern ports, completing the triangle. After the ships were unloaded in Europe, the cycle, which could take a year to complete, began again.

The king's ministers had traditionally been the ones to deal with the colonies on the king's behalf, but as the eighteenth century progressed, Parliament began exercising greater oversight over North America. Initially, laws governing navigation and other acts were accepted as routine regulation of English (and colonial) trade—until Parliament began to appreciate the revenue stream that could come from North America.

In 1733, Parliament passed the Molasses Act. Norwich merchants, like others who sailed to the Caribbean, had been trading as readily in the French, Dutch and Spanish islands as they did in the British West Indies. The Molasses Act taxed molasses and sugar from the French West Indies so heavily that the British islands became the only option for the colonists. The British molasses and sugar were much more expensive than the French, and there was no market in the British islands for the lumber, fish and other products produced in the American colonies. This meant there would be no money coming into the colonies. The law's negative effect on Connecticut and other colonies apparently didn't trouble members of Parliament, who wrote the law as a way to suppress the American colonies, which they viewed as becoming too independent. Americans rarely paid the tax as smuggling became prevalent. In the face of financial ruin, even the most upright merchants and sea captains weren't beyond smuggling or intimidating local officials tasked with collecting the duties. In fact, by 1740, England had given up on enforcing the law. As the Molasses Act reached its expiration date in 1764, Parliament replaced it with the Sugar Act, which cut (but didn't eliminate) the duty on sugar and molasses but also signaled England's intent to enforce the law and collect the taxes owed.

While the American colonies were developing and growing, France was establishing colonies that grew into cities along the St. Lawrence River to the north. Explorers from both nations realized North American wealth was in natural resources, rather than gold. Tall trees would become ships' masts and tar. Wild game had pelts that could be used for many purposes, not least of which were the beaver hats that were then fashionable abroad.

The French *couriers du bois* and others traveled west from Montreal, and English frontiersmen moved inland from the American coast, establishing settlements and building forts to guard them. Inevitably, the two clashed, initially over who would control the area where the Allegheny and Monongahela Rivers meet, at Fort Duquesne (now Pittsburgh, Pennsylvania). Both nations had cultivated alliances with the Native Americans, casting them as allies during the war to come. The fighting began in May 1754 and ended in 1758, when England prevailed. England then determined to control all of French Canada, expanding the war into New York and New England.

The cost was huge, and Parliament reasoned that the North Americans should help pay for the troops that were in North America to protect the English colonists. The colonists resisted, particularly because they had never been consulted about either the war or paying for the troops. Keeping the army in North America solved a domestic problem for Parliament, which would face heavy objections if the troops were recalled to England. Most of the officers, who were from aristocratic families, had no other occupation with which to support themselves. In addition, the English objected to a large

The original thirteen colonies. *Courtesy Library of Congress.*

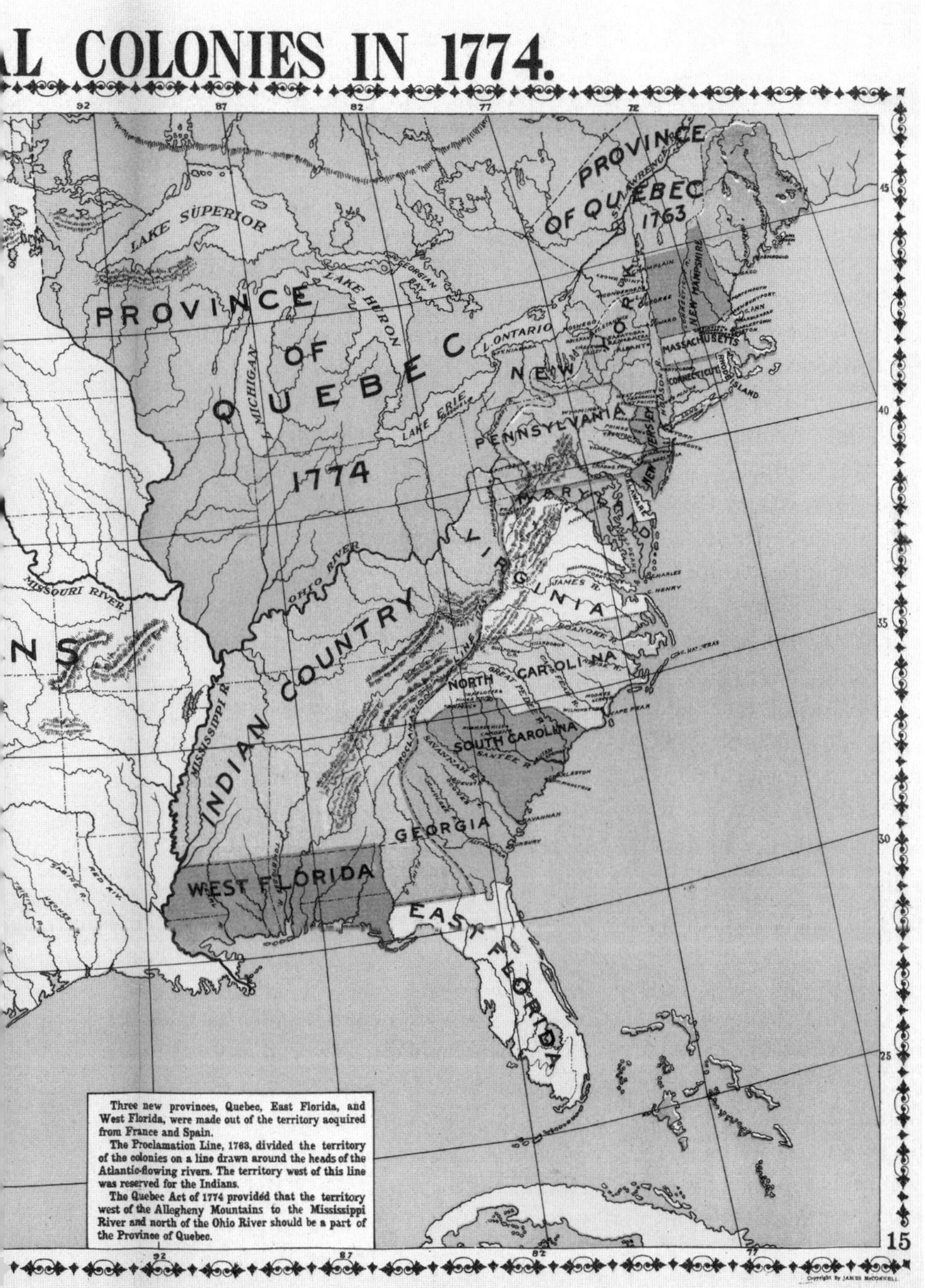
L COLONIES IN 1774.
PROVINCE OF QUEBEC 1763
LAKE SUPERIOR
PROVINCE OF QUEBEC 1774
LAKE MICHIGAN
LAKE HURON
GEORGIAN BAY
L. ONTARIO
LAKE ERIE
NEW YORK
NEW HAMPSHIRE
MASSACHUSETTS
CONNECTICUT
RHODE ISLAND
PENNSYLVANIA
NEW JERSEY
MARYLAND
VIRGINIA
JAMES R.
OHIO RIVER
MISSOURI RIVER
MISSISSIPPI R.
INDIAN COUNTRY
NORTH CAROLINA
SOUTH CAROLINA
SAVANNAH R.
GEORGIA
WEST FLORIDA
EAST FLORIDA
RED RIV.
15
Three new provinces, Quebec, East Florida, and West Florida, were made out of the territory acquired from France and Spain.
The Proclamation Line, 1763, divided the territory of the colonies on a line drawn around the heads of the Atlantic-flowing rivers. The territory west of this line was reserved for the Indians.
The Quebec Act of 1774 providéd that the territory west of the Allegheny Mountains to the Mississippi River and north of the Ohio River should be a part of the Province of Quebec.

standing army at home. Keeping the troops in North America made sense considering the vast amount of territory gained when England defeated France, but it was galling to the colonists, who were expected to pay to solve Parliament's problem. Then, in 1763, the Native American war chief Pontiac launched a war against the British soldiers, who were treating them as lesser beings rather than allies, as the French had. This gave Parliament the justification needed to keep the troops in North America.

England's debt had nearly doubled over the ten years of war with France and the Native Americans, and the new chancellor of the exchequer, Lord George Grenville, launched taxes that would help pay the cost of maintaining the British troops in North America. The Sugar Act passed by Parliament on April 5, 1764, reduced by half the tax on sugar levied by the Molasses Act of 1733, anticipating that increased demand would bring in enough money to make up for the lower duty. Since smuggling had long been an accepted way to avoid the tariff, Parliament included provisions for stricter enforcement. The act also included language that declared the legislation was designed to raise revenue as well as regulate trade. Significantly, the law listed a number of items, most notably lumber, that could be exported only to Britain. This would be regulated by customs officials, who would verify a ship's manifest (the list of the cargo it carried) before anything could be offloaded.

The end of the war damaged the finances of colonials who had been suppliers of the English army. In New England, there was an additional economic hit because smuggling rum had such a narrow profit margin that any price increase to cover the cost of the new tax would seriously damage sales, leaving the rum market to the untaxed producers of the British West Indies. In addition, the prohibition of trade with the West Indies eliminated a source of hard money, which the colonists needed not only for trade but also to pay taxes imposed by England. Furthermore, a lack of hard money destabilized the soundness of the colonial currency.

The first rumblings against the new law were heard in New York and in Boston, where Samuel Adams and James Otis objected to the tax, claiming it violated the colonists' rights as Englishmen. Some merchants said they would stop buying expensive British goods, and both Boston and New York began to work on increasing American manufacturing capability.

Lord Grenville had made it clear more taxes would be forthcoming to meet England's financial needs. In February 1765, he met with Benjamin Franklin and Connecticut's Jared Ingersoll as well as members of Parliament Richard Jackson, who owned land in America and was the agent for Connecticut, and Charles Garth, who served as agent for several Southern colonies. Grenville told them he wanted to raise the money in a way that would be easy and raise the fewest objections among the colonists. He wasn't opposed to letting the colonies decide how to raise the money, but apparently no one had any viable alternative plan beyond letting the Americans decide for themselves, although previous attempts to do so hadn't been successful.

The solution was the Stamp Act, approved by the British Parliament on March 22, 1765. Colonists would pay a direct tax, validated by a stamp affixed to paper goods and documents. Additionally, those who violated the act could be prosecuted in admiralty courts—meaning a trial before a judge, without a jury, which could be held anywhere in the British Empire. This was interpreted to mean that violators could expect to be taken to England for trial.

The reality was that while the colonists viewed the earlier Sugar and Molasses Acts as regulating trade, they saw the Stamp Act as a direct tax on virtually everyone in the colonies. A bill of lading, a newspaper, a diploma, virtually any legal document—even calendars, playing cards and dice—required a stamp. Anyone who filed a deed or took out a mortgage or wanted to probate a will would be affected by the stamp tax. Anyone who took on an indentured servant, the sea captain who was unloading his cargo, lawyers and notaries, newspaper publishers: all were required to have stamps, sometimes one stamp per page of a document. To make matters worse, the stamp tax had to be paid in hard money, not paper currency.

Royal governors told Parliament that the colonies were too disorganized to mount any real objection to the actions of Parliament. Nor did Benjamin Franklin, who was in London, anticipate the outrage from the colonists; in fact, he suggested candidates for the stamp distributor positions. Jared Ingersoll, now acting as a quasi-diplomat, accepted an appointment as stamp distributor, and Norwich's Daniel Lathrop offered his services as assistant. Lathrop may have set his sights on the prospective income rather than considering the political ramifications of the new tax. After the act passed, Lord Grenville promptly began appointing colonial residents as stamp distributors.

The Americans initially accepted Parliament's legislation of trade for the entire empire. The Stamp Act brought a different response: they argued Parliament could not tax the colonies because they were not represented in Parliament. The colonists relied heavily on their rights under the English Constitution. As British citizens, they could be taxed only with their consent, in the form of representation in Parliament. British Members of Parliament George Grenville and Thomas Whately countered that the colonists were like most British citizens who could not vote; they had "virtual representation" in Parliament. Needless to say, the colonists scoffed at that idea, and they weren't alone. Speaking in the House of Commons in 1766, William Pitt characterized it as a "most contemptible" idea that didn't deserve serious consideration. The Americans also argued that colonial legislatures were coequal to Parliament and American allegiance was to the king, placing the colonies beyond Parliamentary reach.

Members of Parliament and the king's ministers also assumed that the colonies would not be able to mount any unified opposition, and even if they did, they would be no match for England. But the colonists' reaction to the Stamp Act was swift and very negative. "No taxation without representation" became their cry. In addition to boycotting British goods, the colonists formed Sons of Liberty groups, whose protests included hanging stamp distributors in effigy and harassing them into giving up the office. In August 1765, in Massachusetts, what was described as a mob burned an effigy of stamp distributor Andrew Oliver, who resigned after they invaded his home and demolished his office.

The colonists formed Committees of Correspondence to report on events and the protest effort, which had the effect of drawing the colonies together. In their first unified act, they called for a Stamp Act Congress, which met in New York in October 1765. Delegates from nine of the thirteen colonies attended; in the others, royal governors or financial considerations intervened to prevent selection of delegates.

For the first time, the colonies acted as a group, in their protest against not only the Stamp Act itself but also a violation of their rights as British citizens—the fact that they could be taxed even though they had no representation in Parliament. In addition, Englishmen who traded with the colonies found themselves affected by the boycott, and they also voiced their objections to Parliament.

The Americans' strong, sometimes violent, reaction to the Stramp Act stopped it before any stamp was ever sold. Parliament repealed the Stamp Act in 1766—but it enacted the Declaratory Act to assert that Parliament's authority was the same in the colonies as it was in Britain and that laws passed by Parliament applied to the colonies "in all cases whatsoever." And when the colonies fought back, Norwich residents were heavily involved.

CHAPTER 2

JOHN DURKEE (1728–1782)

HONORABLE, PRINCIPLED, BOLD

When America declared its independence from England, John Durkee found himself in the unenviable position of defending his new country against men who had been his friends and comrades in arms only a few years before. Durkee was among the American patriots who served in His Majesty's army before joining the Continentals.

At thirty-nine, Durkee was a veteran of the French and Indian Wars, a merchant, farmer, justice of the peace and keeper of a tavern and inn, according to Dayne Rugh, author of *John Durkee: The Forgotten Story of Connecticut's Bold Man from Bean Hill*, a biography of Durkee published in 2024. John Durkee's story began on December 11, 1728, in Windham, Connecticut, in the town we now know as Hampton. His parents were Susannah Sabin and William Durkee, whose ancestor William Durkee (also spelled Durgy) was an Irish soldier who was sent to Barbados as an indentured servant after being captured by Cromwell's soldiers. His indenture was turned over to Thomas Bishop, who brought him to Ipswich, Massachusetts. William Durkee is believed to have been the first Irish Catholic in Massachusetts. He married Martha Cross, an Ipswich girl and a Protestant, who raised their children as Protestants. The family later moved to Windham, Connecticut. Both of their sons became Protestant ministers, and their grandson William (John Durkee's father) was a deacon of the church in Windham.

John Durkee moved to Norwich sometime before 1746, when he took out a loan to buy a parcel of land near Bean Hill. Rugh puts the location at about where Route 395 intersects West Town Street. In addition to farming,

Durkee operated an inn and tavern. He was also a merchant and later served as a justice of the peace. On January 3, 1753, Durkee married Norwich resident Martha Wood, with whom he had four children. They had about three peaceful years before John felt compelled to enlist in the British army to fight against the French in the war over who would control North America.

In May 1756, Durkee was commissioned a second lieutenant in the Second Regiment, commanded by Colonel David Wooster. They were among the Connecticut troops led by General Phineas Lyman of Durham. By July, Durkee was at Fort Edward in upstate New York preparing to take Crown Point and other sites on Lake Champlain. Rather than fighting, they spent the summer building up the defenses at Fort Edward and nearby Fort William Henry. Durkee returned to Norwich in November 1756 and resumed his life as a farmer, tavernkeeper and father to his three-year-old daughter, Anna. In February 1757, he was again commissioned, as a first lieutenant this time, and by April, he was marching toward New York with Lyman's troops.

Sergeant Jabez Fitch of Bozrah kept a journal that has become a record of events during the campaign. The soldiers again worked at strengthening defenses and making repairs at the fort, and on June 11, they had their first exposure to the brutality of this war. Rugh describes how they heard gunshots around eleven o'clock in the morning and found General Lyman and others chasing enemy attackers, who left four soldiers dead and five missing. The dead had been mutilated. On July 4, they found the body of another soldier: he had been scalped, his throat cut and his heart cut from his chest. It's hard to imagine standing guard duty knowing that would be your fate if you were captured, yet Durkee and the others stood their posts.

By August, the French had surrounded Fort William Henry. A call for reinforcements went out across New England, and Connecticut quickly responded. Unfortunately, by the time the fresh troops arrived, it was too late. The British were evacuating the fort, and the French were supposed to release any captives or soldiers who remained. Instead, their Native allies ransacked the fort and killed as many as two hundred, including soldiers who were sick and wounded.

Although he had been discharged, Durkee, newly promoted to captain, elected to stay on at Fort Edward through the winter and personally invited Fitch to remain with him and some of the other soldiers. Sergeant Fitch described a scene on Christmas Day 1757, when he and Durkee shared some sweets and chocolate and then spent the end of the day in front of the fire with some of the others. Fitch heard a noise, went to investigate and found a fire in one of the barracks. Their quiet evening promptly ended in fighting the fire, which they extinguished before it reached the nearby powder magazine.

By the spring of 1758, Captain Durkee was in command of the Ninth Company, Third Regiment. Although they were 250 miles from Norwich, Durkee found himself surrounded by "home." Rugh notes that the regimental commander, Colonel Eleazer Fitch, hailed from Windham. Among Durkee's officers, Lieutenants Eleazer Tracy, Joseph Bingham and Ensign Daniel Hyde Jr. were all Norwich boys. Rugh's list of others in the company includes Captain Durkee's distant cousin Bartholomew Durkee and Native American and African American soldiers, including "Negroe Coff," "Negroe Cesar" and Zachariah Wauquandum, who was apparently a member of the Pequot tribe.

Torrential rains that destroyed buildings and huts (including Durkee's), followed by Indian attacks that killed a dozen British soldiers, left the discouraged Connecticut men ready to head home. To Major Israel Putnam fell the task of telling them it was out of the question. No one, he told them, could leave camp unless their enlistment had expired. Sergeant Fitch recorded the response of the soldiers as "the most dreadful rage." There were some lighter moments, such as a March evening spent playing cards after a good dinner, but pleasantries were quickly canceled by another attack, more dead soldiers and more wounded to nurse.

An entry in Sergeant Fitch's diary indicates that Captain Durkee was able to get home for a visit that spring. He apparently was back in New York for the events of a disheartening summer that included an unsuccessful attempt to take Fort Ticonderoga and the battlefield death of the British commander General Lord George Howe, who was well liked by the colonials. General Lyman wrote of his discouragement to Connecticut Governor Jonathan Trumbull, a close friend.

The appointment of Lord Jeffrey Amherst as commanding general of the British forces in North America brought rapid change. He captured Louisburg on the Nova Scotia coast before the end of the year. Durkee returned to the fighting in the spring of 1759 as major of the Third Company of Eleazer Fitch's Fourth Regiment of Provincials.

By July, the army had captured Fort Ticonderoga and engaged in a siege of Quebec, Canada. Durkee and his men made a thirty-four-day march to Fort Oswego and then to the shores of Lake Ontario. From there, they marched to Montreal, which was surrendered on September 8, 1760, after a two-day siege. This ended French dominance in Canada and allowed

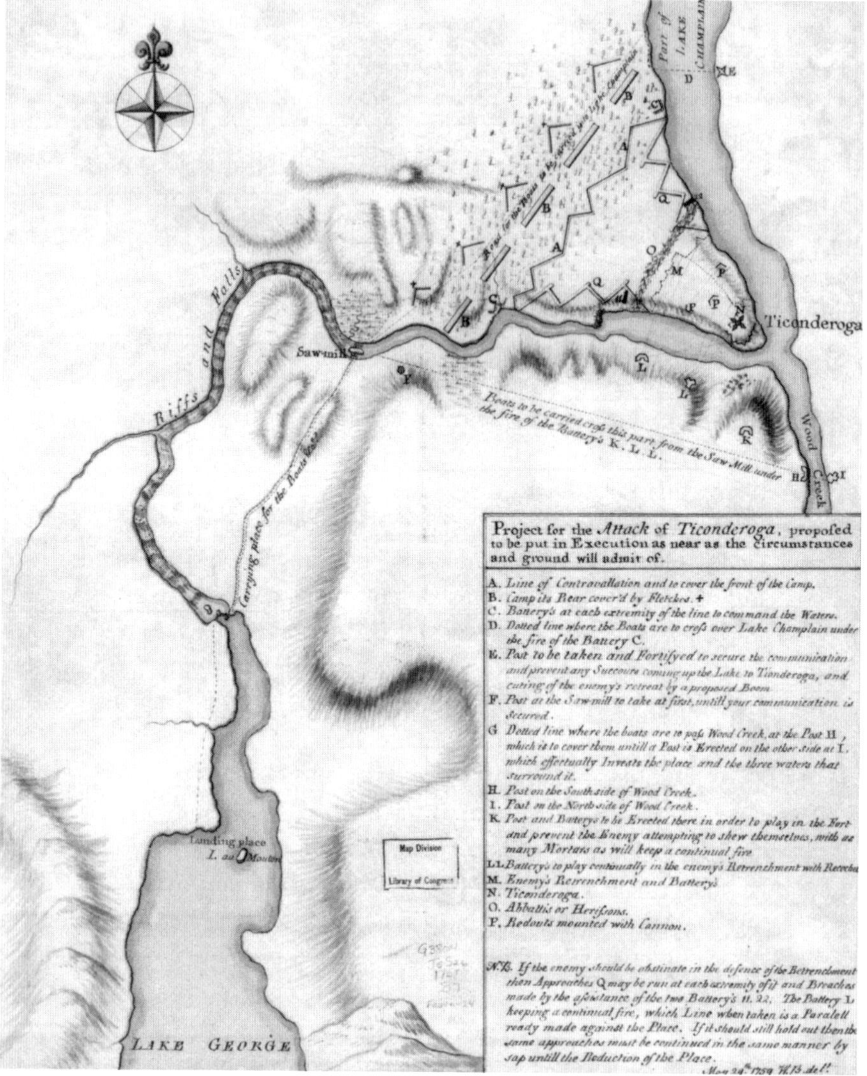

Fort Ticonderoga and the surrounding area. *Courtesy Library of Congress.*

Durkee to return to Norwich. That didn't last, however, as in 1761, Durkee answered General Lyman's call to enlist. He found himself back in upstate New York, doing construction work to reinforce various military sites. He wrote to his wife in September that he hoped to be home in November.

Yet one more call to arms was issued in 1762. Lord Amherst requested militia from certain states, and in June, two thousand Provincials boarded ships in New York bound for Havana, Cuba. It was a difficult, hazardous trip, but when they arrived in Havana Harbor, they were greeted by the masts of two hundred ships. Fifteen thousand soldiers were nearby. In mid-August, Major Durkee was among the soldiers who entered the fortress of El Morro after repeated bombardments from the British guns. A large amount of cash and other valuables was seized, and Durkee found himself entitled to a share of the prize money that was distributed among the officers and soldiers. It was December before Durkee was back in Norwich, where he received a hero's welcome. He also met for the first time his third child, a boy, named Phineas Allen after his father's commanding officer.

In *To the Beat of a Drum*, Norwich historian Nafie describes Norwich as a "hotbed of radicalism" that was "on the verge of revolt" as early as 1765. Sons of Liberty groups began forming in Boston and New York. They soon connected with groups in neighboring colonies and set up a correspondence chain to keep each other apprised of local events. Durkee was the leader of the Norwich Sons of Liberty, who spearheaded the town's strong negative response to England's attempts to impose the 1765 stamp tax on the colonists.

When Jared Ingersoll, now a New Haven lawyer, was commissioned as Connecticut's stamp agent, Norwich responded on August 21, 1765: Ingersoll was burned in effigy on the Norwichtown Green. Ingersoll had previously refused to resign until he consulted the Connecticut General Assembly. In September, Durkee learned that Ingersoll was going to Hartford. He contacted his friend and former comrade-in-arms Captain Zebulon Butler of New London. Between them they raised five hundred men, who packed eight days' provisions and rode toward Hartford. As they rode, men from other towns joined them until the group numbered about one thousand by the time they arrived in Wethersfield.

On September 19, they intercepted Ingersoll and assembled on the present-day Broad Street Green. Although surrounded by angry men, some of whom were armed, Ingersoll refused to resign. They took him to a nearby tavern and might have kept him there for some time. At least one account had the mob offering Ingersoll a choice: jail or hanging. Ingersoll decided the cause was "not worth dying for" and agreed to resign, prompting cheers from the crowd. The mob escorted Ingersoll to the statehouse to ensure he repeated his resignation before the assembly. That autumn, a liberty pole, complete with cap at its top, appeared on the Norwichtown Green. These poles were a symbol of dissent against England.

Like those of many others, Durkee's farm and his business interests suffered from England's increasing demands on the colonies. With two

The Norwichtown Green in colonial times. The liberty pole is shown near the tip of the Green. *Courtesy Slater Memorial Museum.*

HISTORIC NORWICHTOWN GREEN
1775–1784

OUSE
OUSE
R SHOP

8. AZARIAH LATHROP HOUSE
*9. JOHN PERIT HOUSE
*10. JOHN PERIT'S STORE
*11. COURTHOUSE
*12. WHIPPING POST AND PILLORY
13. DIAH MANNING HOUSE
14. LORD TAVERN
*15. REV. BENJAMIN LORD HOUSE
*16. LATHROP TAVERN
*17. MEETINGHOUSE
*18. POWDER HOUSE
*19. DUDLEY WOODBRIDGE'S STORE
*20. DUDLEY WOODBRIDGE HOUSE
21. BROWN'S TAVERN
22. JOSEPH CARPENTER SILVERSMITH SHOP
23. SCHOOLHOUSE
*24. SETH MINER HOUSE
*25. JAIL
*26. NATHANIEL PATTEN BOOKSTORE
*27. WILLIAM LAX'S SHOP
*28. DARIUS PECK'S SHOP
*29. DARIUS PECK HOUSE
30. CHARLTON FAMILY HOUSE
31. CHARLTON FAMILY HOUSE
32. PARMENAS JONES HOUSE
*33. BENJAMIN BUTLER'S BLACKSMITH SHOP
*34. DAVID ROGERS HOUSE
*35. BENJAMIN BUTLER HOUSE
*36. HUNTINGTON DISTILLERY
37. WHITING HOUSE

*RAZED

ELM AVENUE
TOWN STREET
N
C. Nagle '74
← WEST TOWN STREET

friends, merchant Durkee acquired a sloop, expecting to trade along the coast and in the West Indies. The English restrictions on trade and imposition of tariffs led to increasing financial difficulties that even commonly accepted smuggling wouldn't overcome. Tariffs on sugar, requirements that taxes be paid in hard money and other British laws had a negative impact on colonial merchants.

In 1767, Durkee was named to a committee of the town's "most prominent inhabitants" to draft a response to the Massachusetts Circular Letter recommending that colonists stop using or buying things produced in England. According to Caulkins, the finished document, written "in conformity with the noble example set by Boston," was an agreement not to import, buy or use tea, wine, spirits (alcoholic beverages) and nearly all items made outside of the colonies, with a few exceptions. The authors "strongly recommended" that the women of the town "omit tea-drinking in the afternoon" and suggested that militia officers scale back the "lavish and extravagant entertainments" they were accustomed to giving for their companies following their election as officers. Presumably, this was an appeal to stop serving imported wine and liquors and stick to hard cider, beer and rum that could be produced in the colonies. Considering that Durkee was the proprietor of a tavern, there was probably some sacrifice in what the committee was urging. The same year, Durkee found it necessary to mortgage his properties, including his home. Perhaps that was the impetus for his next great adventure.

A little over a decade earlier, a group of eastern Connecticut men organized the Susquehanna Company with the intent of settling along the Susquehanna River in Pennsylvania. They apparently reasoned that a century earlier, the original Connecticut Charter of 1662 extended the colony's borders to the westernmost edge of the continent. (Basically, extend the lines of the Massachusetts border and Long Island Sound west to the Pacific Ocean: that land belongs to Connecticut.) With the charter, the king granted

> *ALL that parte of our dominions in Newe England in America bounded on the East by Norrogancett River, commonly called Norrogancett Bay, where the said River falleth into the Sea, and on the North by the lyne of the Massachusetts Plantacon, and on the south by the Sea, and in longitude as the lyne of the Massachusetts Colony, runinge from East to West, (that is to say) from the Said Norrogancett Bay on the East to the South Sea on the West parte, with the Islands thervnto adioyneinge, Together with all firme lands…TO HAVE AND TO HOLD…for ever.*

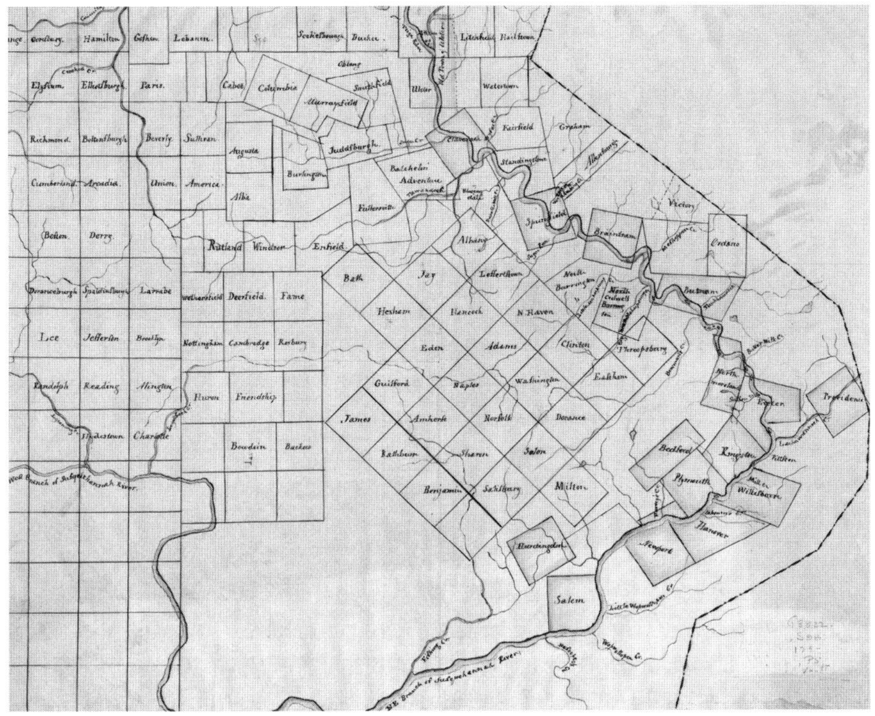

John Durkee helped draw this map of the Susquehanna settlement. *Courtesy Library of Congress.*

The prospective Susquehanna settlers spent the next decade caught between Pennsylvania, Connecticut and Native American tribes as they tried to establish legitimate ownership of a tract of land in the Wyoming Valley of Pennsylvania. Although their agent had bought the land from Native Americans of the Six Nations, the Natives apparently were inebriated at the time, placing the deed and ownership of the land in question. The French and Indian War interrupted plans for settlement, but the end of the hostilities prompted the Susquehanna investors to go forward.

Parliament's Proclamation of 1763 that banned colonial settlement beyond the Allegheny Mountains included much of the land claimed by the Susquehanna group, which by then included Durkee, who held a half share of the company stock. In 1768, a new treaty opened the land for settlement, and in December, the Connecticut group announced their plan to send forty men and then another two hundred to settle their claim. Connecticut officials were divided on extending the state's borders.

Pennsylvania had strong objections to what it considered an incursion, and the group was ordered to leave. They were arrested, but their response was to send out more settlers; this time John Durkee was a leader of the group of 146. When another 150 men arrived soon after, the group outnumbered the Pennsylvanians in the area and commenced building cottages for a permanent settlement. The fortress was named Fort Durkee in honor of their leader.

The Pennsylvania government pursued its court cases as the Connecticut settlers planted crops and named the settlement Wilkes-Barre, for Sir John Wilkes and Sir Isaac Barre, members of Parliament who opposed the Stamp Act. Barre was among the British soldiers who served with Durkee during the French and Indian War.

In November 1769, Durkee was arrested and taken in shackles to Philadelphia. Meanwhile, the Pennsylvanians took advantage of his absence, and two hundred armed men surrounded the fort, ultimately forcing abandonment of Fort Durkee. After two weeks in wretched conditions at the Philadelphia jail, Durkee was released on bail and returned to Norwich. The Susquehanna Company investors were determined to continue their settlement efforts. Although there was yet another skirmish with Pennsylvania authorities, the Susquehanna settlers were able to lay out the plan for a town, establish a trading post and recruit a minister.

In June, Pennsylvania's governor proclaimed the Fort Durkee inhabitants a threat to public safety and ordered them to leave, although warrants weren't issued until September. Pennsylvania sheriffs arrived to arrest Durkee and several of the others. Durkee was again confined to the harsh conditions of the Philadelphia jail, this time for nearly two years, as the states argued about ownership of the Susquehanna land. Thanks to his supporters, Durkee was finally released, and he returned home in August 1772. His health was seriously compromised because of the poor conditions in the jail. The issue of ownership wasn't settled until after the War for Independence ended, when a court ruled that the land belonged to Pennsylvania but the individual ownership claims of Connecticut men should be honored.

It seems safe to assume Durkee did what he could over the following months as resistance to English rule grew in the colonies. In August 1774, he mustered almost five hundred men in response to reports of fighting near Boston. As they reached the nearby town of Lisbon, they encountered David Nevins, who had ridden all night with the news that the report from Boston was a false alarm. There was nothing for Durkee and his men to do but turn their horses back to Norwich.

Eight months later, Durkee led his Norwich militiamen to Boston in response to an express rider who carried firsthand reports of the fighting at Concord and Lexington. In the ranks were his sons, seventeen-year-old Private John Durkee Jr. and twelve-year-old Phineas, a fifer. They joined Israel Putnam, now a major general, at Charlestown on the north side of Boston. There, they helped build redoubts at what we now call Bunker Hill, in anticipation of further fighting with the British army. On the morning of June 17, 1775, the British army awoke to find colonial troops entrenched atop the heights of Charlestown. Putnam and Durkee would have been looking down at the British and perhaps wrestling with the idea that they might soon be shooting at men they knew well, men they fought beside ten or fifteen years before.

When the maneuvering was over and the battle began, Durkee's men and the other Americans proved deadly in their aim through two British attacks. Red coats covering shattered bodies lay across the hillside, and the British fell back. After the third attack, the colonists had exhausted their ammunition supply and were forced to retreat. The British claimed the ground, but at the cost of one thousand casualties, including eighty-one officers killed or wounded. The Americans counted four hundred casualties. From nearby Roxbury, Samuel Gray wrote to Eliphalet Dyer that Durkee and his men "did honor to themselves and the cause of their country." Gray and Dyer were both Windham officials who would have been well acquainted with Durkee, both as a former Windham resident and, in Dyer's case, as a former comrade-in-arms at Fort Ticonderoga. At the time, Dyer was a delegate to the Continental Congress.

With the arrival of General George Washington, Durkee and his men became part of General Putnam's regiment in the Continental army. The British became thoroughly ensconced in Boston, surrounded by American troops. At that time, Boston was a peninsula, and the only access was a narrow strip of land, called the Neck, that connected it to the mainland town of Roxbury. By blocking the Roxbury end of the Neck, the American army was able to keep the British from leaving by land, and American ships prevented British supply ships from reaching Boston. The British army posted guards on the Boston side of the neck, so neither people nor regular commerce could get into Boston. In January 1776, Henry Knox arrived with cannons seized at Fort Ticonderoga, New York. Knox had spent nearly two months hauling the cannons overland across New York and Massachusetts through bitter winter conditions. Supplies of musket balls and powder arrived a few weeks later. On the night of March 4, Washington ordered the

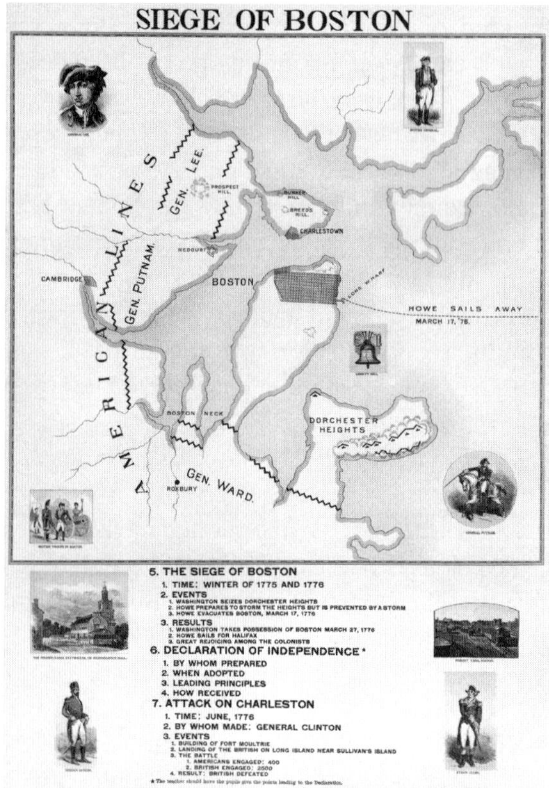

The British view of the defenses around Boston in 1775–76. *Courtesy Library of Congress.*

cannons placed on top of Dorchester Heights on the south side of the city, overlooking Boston Harbor and the British ships moored there. For a second time, the British awoke to find cannon aimed at them.

Although General William Howe scheduled an attack, it was thwarted by a snowstorm, and he declined to try again. Finally, on March 17, 1776, British troops began boarding ships bound for Newfoundland. That date is still celebrated as Evacuation Day, a legal holiday in Boston.

After the British departure from Boston, General Washington believed Howe would set his sights on New York, so Durkee and his men marched with the army southwest across Connecticut. Washington reorganized the army, promoting Durkee to lieutenant colonel of the Twentieth Continentals, assigned to the army's Second Brigade.

In New York, a plot that threatened Washington's life was uncovered. Durkee, his fellow townsman Jedidiah Huntington and other officers of the Second Brigade wrote to Washington, denouncing the plot and assuring him of their loyalty both to him and to the cause.

Durkee was sent to New Jersey to find and repair small boats that could be used to transport Washington's troops. On July 9, Durkee and his men were likely among the troops Washington assembled in New York to hear a reading of the Declaration of Independence, which had been adopted by the Continental Congress five days before.

Durkee was soon back in New Jersey to establish a defensive position, and a few weeks later, British ships landed thirty-two thousand soldiers on Staten Island across from Durkee's position. Washington moved his soldiers to Manhattan, and in the early hours of August 29, Durkee's men covered the army's retreat across the East River, presumably on the small boats they acquired when they first arrived in New York.

Over the next few weeks, the British bombarded Durkee's position, and his men returned fire. When the regulars landed at his Paulus Hook position, Washington ordered them to join the main army in Manhattan. Over the next few months, the Americans suffered losses at White Plains and Forts Washington and Lee before retreating to Pennsylvania. Morale was very low, and many men expected to leave the army when their enlistment expired at the end of the year.

Early in December, Thomas Paine published his pamphlet *The American Crisis*, which began:

> *THESE are the times that try men's souls. The summer soldier and the sunshine patriot will, in this crisis, shrink from the service of their country; but he that stands by it now, deserves the love and thanks of man and woman. Tyranny, like hell, is not easily conquered; yet we have this consolation with us, that the harder the conflict, the more glorious the triumph. What we obtain too cheap, we esteem too lightly: it is dearness only that gives everything its value. Heaven knows how to put a proper price upon its goods; and it would be strange indeed if so celestial an article as FREEDOM should not be highly rated.*

Paine's pamphlet was widely shared among the soldiers and gave them what they needed to stay for one last effort. On Christmas night 1776, Washington led his army across the Delaware River in a blinding snowstorm to attack a garrison of Hessian soldiers and supply depot in Trenton, New Jersey. Their success raised morale and led to another victory at Princeton, New Jersey, ten days later.

During much of 1777, the British army remained in control of Philadelphia, and the fighting in New Jersey was a series of relatively minor battles. The major action was in the north, culminating with a September victory at Saratoga that gave France the impetus to enter the war on the American side.

In December 1777, the army went into winter quarters at Valley Forge, where the soldiers endured bitter cold and shortages of rations, supplies and adequate shelter. The conditions may have struck Durkee as eerily similar to what he had experienced twenty years before at Fort Edward.

In the new year, the recently arrived Baron Friedrich von Steuben, a former Prussian army officer, was appalled at the conditions he found and began drilling the men and teaching them military-style fighting. The result of von Steuben's efforts was apparent as soon as the Continental army took the field that spring.

British General Henry Clinton, who replaced General William Howe, evacuated Philadelphia on June 18, 1778. Washington's army harassed his troops with small skirmishes as they marched across New Jersey to Sandy Hook, where ships waited to take the army to New York.

Colonel Durkee and his men marched with General Charles Lee, who had just returned to the army after an extended incarceration as a prisoner of war. Washington's plan was for Lee and his five thousand troops to strike the British rear guard without precipitating a major engagement. When they neared the British army, Lee ordered Durkee to station his men at the rear of wetlands near Spottswood Brook in Monmouth Courthouse. Lee discovered far too late that the British rear guard was larger than expected. The British began firing on the Continentals in what was to be the three-hour Battle of Monmouth, filling the area with smoke and heat from the guns and intensifying the effects of temperatures recorded at over one hundred degrees. Communications were confusing, and ultimately, Lee ordered his troops to retreat.

When Washington arrived with the main army, he thought Lee's troops were advancing on the British, leaving him angry when he discovered the opposite. According to biographer Rugh, Washington ordered some of Lee's troops, likely including Durkee's men, to attack the British rear guard in a small orchard near Perine Hill. This is probably where Colonel Durkee was injured when a musket ball went through his right hand and shrapnel hit his left hand.

The effect of von Steuben's winter drills became apparent as the Americans remained steady in the face of British bayonet attacks. The armies exchanged artillery fire for two hours, until the Americans established an artillery position on a hill and Clinton began withdrawing. Washington continued attacking as they retreated, causing heavy casualties. Sunset provided the cover Clinton needed to slip away and reach New York without additional fighting. Although the battle was technically a draw, the Americans remained in control of the battlefield, allowing Washington to claim a victory, which raised confidence and spirits not just in the army but also in Congress.

For his part, the seriously injured Durkee returned to Norwich, where he remained on leave from combat duty for the rest of 1778. He spent the next couple of years gathering intelligence, recruiting and tending to administrative matters for the army, not knowing that his fighting days were over.

In early September 1780, Durkee received a letter about administrative matters from Norwich native General Benedict Arnold, then commandant of the fort at West Point, New York. On September 9, 1780, Durkee responded and closed by writing, "I should be happy to see you." Twelve days later, Arnold defected to the British. Since he was twelve years older, Durkee would not have known Arnold especially well, but it's easy to imagine his shock and perhaps horror when he learned of Arnold's treason. Despite the difference in age, their backgrounds were fairly similar, and it's likely Durkee was unable to understand why Arnold would abandon their country after fighting for it for so long.

Durkee continued working on administrative tasks and overseeing courts-martial through 1781. He clung to the hope he could return to active duty and receive a promotion to general, but his ill health and injuries made it impossible. Several generals, including Norwich's Jedidiah Huntington, urged Washington to make some provision for Durkee, but apparently nothing came of the effort.

Thus, John Durkee remained Colonel Durkee until his death on May 29, 1782, at age fifty-four. He was buried in the Old Colonial Burying Ground with military honors befitting a hero.

Chapter 3

CHRISTOPHER LEFFINGWELL (1734–1810)

Entrepreneur, Provisioner, Patriot

If you needed something—supplies, a ship, paper, stockings, chocolate—Christopher Leffingwell either had it, could make it or could find it. As one of Connecticut's first manufacturers, he made the paper, stockings and chocolate. For the other items, General George Washington and Governor Jonathan Trumbull turned to Leffingwell to supply the army.

Leffingwell was born in Norwich in 1734 to Benajah and Joanna (Christopher) Leffingwell. His great-grandfather Thomas Leffingwell was one of the founders of Norwich. It was Thomas Leffingwell who delivered food to Uncas and members of the Mohegan Nation as they were besieged by the Narragansetts in 1645, cementing a relationship that led to the purchase of the nine-mile-by-nine-mile square that became Norwich.

Little is known about Leffingwell's early years, but the city's historians have determined that the Leffingwells were a well-to-do family. The wills of family members listed silver spoons, gold coins and land among their assets. Christopher's father was probably a merchant, as he had a shop and owned a ship and also property (most likely a wharf) at the Norwich Landing. When Benajah Leffingwell died in 1756, he left two shares of his estate to Christopher as his eldest son; the other children had one share each. The will stipulated that Benajah's lands were to benefit the children until they turned twenty-one.

Christopher Leffingwell married Elizabeth Harris of New London in 1760. They had two daughters, apparently twins born overnight, as their birth dates were recorded a day apart. Elizabeth died shortly after her birth;

the other, called Beth, died when she was two years old, followed shortly after by her mother. In 1764, Christopher married Elizabeth Coit, daughter of Joseph and Elizabeth Coit of New London. They had ten children.

By 1766, Leffingwell had established a stocking-weaving business. Caulkins described it as "under the patronage of Christopher Leffingwell" with William Russell as the first operator. Over the next twenty-five years, the operation grew to nine looms and five operators, who turned out 1,200 to 1,500 pairs of silk, worsted cotton and linen stockings annually. In addition, it produced gloves and purses.

Leffingwell and John Bliss established Connecticut's first paper mill in 1766 in the first of his shops built along the Yantic River near the intersection of today's Washington Street and Harland Road. Eventually, the area became known as Leffingwell Row. The mill produced paper for writing and wrapping as well as papers for cartridges. In addition, Leffingwell's mill produced the paper for two local newspapers, the *Norwich Packet* and the *New London Gazette*. Caulkins recorded annual production of as much as 1,300 reams, which sold for four to forty-five shillings a ream. She added that the mill was a source of both great excitement and curiosity in the community.

In 1770, Christopher and his brother Elisha opened the first chocolate mill in Norwich, with annual production of as much as four thousand to five thousand pounds of fine-quality chocolate that sold for about nine dollars a pound wholesale and just over eleven dollars a pound retail, making this a lucrative pursuit. Another business was the Leffingwell tavern, housed in the building known today as the Leffingwell House Museum, which was relocated to its present site in the 1950s when the Route 2 highway was constructed. Also in 1770, Leffingwell opened a fulling mill to felt wool after cleaning it in preparation for finishing and an attached dyehouse.

As Leffingwell was a merchant, his finances would certainly have been affected by the taxes Parliament enacted during the 1760s, but he was able to operate his businesses and acquire substantial real estate, and by 1770, he was regarded as one of the town's leading citizens.

In March 1774, Parliament passed a law closing the Port of Boston as retaliation for the Boston Tea Party. No ships could land or depart until colonists had paid for of the 340 chests of tea dumped into Boston Harbor the previous December. Word of the new law reached America within two months, and by June, the outraged colonists had begun organizing.

The Norwich Town Meeting appointed Leffingwell to a committee charged with expressing Norwich's objections to the British action. He was also appointed a member of the Norwich Committee of Correspondence.

Christopher Leffingwell's house as it appeared around 1960. *Courtesy National Parks Service/HABS.*

These committees were modeled on the Boston Committee organized by Samuel Adams and others as a means of disseminating information among colonies but also as a vehicle for gathering support for the patriot cause. He also was the appointed naval officer for the port.

In April 1775, when British regulars clashed with American minutemen at Lexington and Concord in Massachusetts, express rider Israel Bissell delivered a written account of the fighting to Worcester, where the document was copied and sent on to Connecticut. At Brooklyn, Connecticut, Captain Daniel Tyler copied the letter to be sent on to Norwich and then prepared to leave for Boston with his father-in-law, General Israel Putnam.

The Lexington Alarm letter was addressed to Christopher Leffingwell, who received it at his home in Norwich.

> *Watertown Wednesday Morning near 10 O'Clock*
>
> *To all the Friends of American Liberty, be it known that this Morning before breake of Day a Brigade consisting of about 1000 or 1200 Men landed at Phip's Farm at Cambridge & marched to Lexington where they found a Company of our Colony Militia in Arms, upon Whom they fired without any Provocation and killed 6 Men and Wounded 4 others. By an Express from Boston this Moment, we find another Brigade are now upon*

their march from Boston supposed to be about 1000. The Bearer Mr. Israel Bissel is charged to alarm the Country quite to Connecticut and all Persons are desired to furnish him with Fresh Horses as they may be needed. I have spoken with Several Persons who have seen the Dead & Wounded. Pray let the Delegates from this Colony to Connecticut see this they know.

J. Palmer, one of the Committee of S—y [i.e. Safety].

Col. Foster of Brookfield one of the Delegates. A True Coppy taken from the original p[er] *order of Committee of Correspondence for Worcester.*

Attest. Nathan Balding T[own] *Clerk Worcester April 19TH, 1775.*

Brooklyne Thursday 11 o'Clock—The above is a true Coppy as rec[eived] *here p*[er] *Express forwarded from Worcester*—[at]*Test. Daniel Tyler, Jr.*

First Alarm April 1775
To Christopher Leffingwell Esq
or Either the Committee of Correspondence
Norwich

After he read the letter, Leffingwell had it copied and added the following:

Norwich, Thursday 4 o'clock, above is a true copy as by express from Mr. Tyler. Attest. Christopher Leffingwell.

The notations trace Bissell's journey as each recipient made a "true copy" of the letter, which was sent on to the next town until his trip ended in Philadelphia. Interestingly, the Leffingwell House website notes that

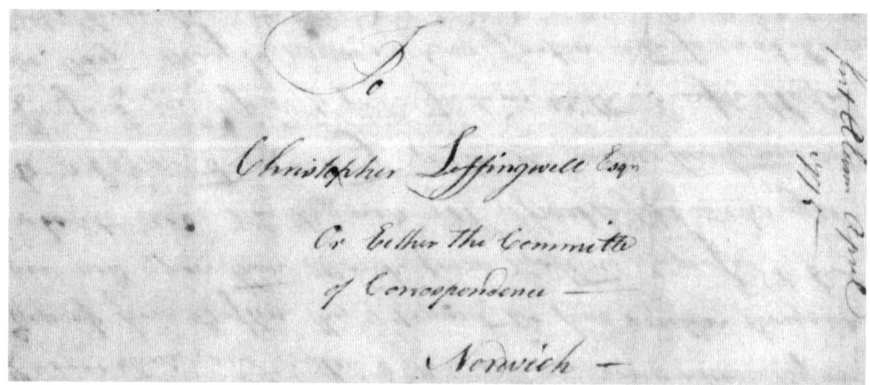

To
Christopher Leffingwell Esqr
Or Either the Committe
of Correspondence —
Norwich —

First Alarm April 1775

The Lexington Alarm letter addressed to Christopher Leffingwell in April 1775. *Courtesy Leffingwell House Museum/Society of the Founders of Norwich.*

Leffingwell's mill produced the paper on which the alarm letter was written. The original letter is in the collection of the Scottish Rite Masonic Museum & Library in Lexington, Massachusetts.

A few weeks later, Christopher Leffingwell met with Silas Dean and other prominent Connecticut men to discuss ways to aid Boston. They also launched a plan to capture the armaments and ammunition stored at Fort Ticonderoga and Crown Point in New York. Mott was ordered to carry out the expedition, and Leffingwell required him to keep a journal of his activity.

Leffingwell had been appointed deputy commissary for the army. Over the next six months, at the behest of Commissary General Joseph Trumbull, much of Leffingwell's activity centered on obtaining supplies for the army: blankets and firelocks in June, uniforms from Montreal, pork to feed the soldiers and molasses. Over the summer of 1775, bakers in Norwich and New London baked bread for the soldiers who were passing through Norwich on their way to New York. At one point, Leffingwell predicted that ten more regiments were expected. Like the other supporters of the American cause, Leffingwell found himself struggling to pay for the needed supplies. Paper money had little value, and the hard money farmers expected in payment was scarce.

Leffingwell's activities during the war weren't confined to finding supplies. By the late summer of 1776, the Committee of Safety had ordered him to bring refugees from Long Island to Connecticut. The now-Colonel Leffingwell mustered a company of infantry and sailed to Southold. Over two days, they boarded families and their belongings as well as 500 sheep and 200 head of cattle and sailed back to New London. A few days later, Leffingwell, with two ships, made a second trip for more families and their furniture, 790 sheep and 152 head of horned cattle. This time, they sailed to Norwich, where the families and their property would be reunited.

Like many others, Leffingwell paid a price for his patriotism. It took three years for him to be paid the £130 New York owed him for transporting the Southold residents. Meanwhile, he turned to privateering, apparently in hopes of covering at least some of his losses. He took shares in several ships, probably in an attempt to spread his financial risk. Leffingwell ships were sailing to Boston, New York, Maryland and Virginia as well as France and Holland. But again, his patriotism came at a personal cost. A state agent chartered Leffingwell's ship *Polly* to sail to the West Indies for supplies. Finding the Port of New London blockaded when it returned, the ship sailed to Boston at the direction of Connecticut Governor Trumbull to store its cargo. Leffingwell wanted the ship returned to Norwich, but unbeknownst to him, the governor ordered *Polly* to make another voyage to the West Indies. This time, it was captured, leaving Leffingwell to demand reimbursement of its full value, which he set at £795.

After the war, life began to return to normal. Leffingwell resumed his business activities and continued his government service as supervisor of the Port of Norwich and colonel of the Norwich Light Infantry Brigade. In 1785, Leffingwell was appointed a state agent to oversee the sale of the state's stock of saltpeter and sulfur, key ingredients in making gunpowder. He was directed to obtain the best possible price.

Elizabeth Coit Leffingwell, Christopher's second wife, died in 1796. He married Ruth Perit of New Haven in 1799. Christopher Leffingwell died at the age of seventy-six on November 7, 1810. He is buried in the Old Colonial Burying Ground in Norwichtown.

Chapter 4

JEDIDIAH HUNTINGTON (1743–1818)

"Your Excellency's Most Obedient Servant"

Jedidiah Huntington was an unlikely soldier. He was the son of a wealthy merchant, born into one of the leading families of Norwich, well educated, married with a family. Yet he joined the militia, rose through the officers' ranks and eventually became a general. He endured the stifling heat and the brutal cold, the driving rain and the noise and confusion and fear of battle in the cause of liberty.

Jedidiah was born on August 4, 1743, the eldest child of Jabez and Elizabeth (Backus) Huntington. His brother Andrew was born a month before their mother's death in 1845. Jabez remarried a year later to Hannah Williams of Pomfret, and they had six children: Joshua, Hannah, Ebenezer, Elizabeth, Mary and Zachariah.

Although little is known about Jedidiah's early years, it is on record that he went to Harvard College and graduated in 1763. Class rankings at that time were dictated by the wealth of the students' families, and Jedidiah Huntington was second in his class. In 1763, he married Faith Trumbull, whose father was a prominent merchant and politician and became Connecticut's governor in 1769. Jedidiah earned a master's degree from Yale in 1770 and then became a merchant himself, joining his father in business, which included a fleet of ships that traded in the Caribbean. He joined the militia as well and became active in Norwich's Sons of Liberty. In 1774, Jedidiah was among the Norwich men named to the town's Committee of Correspondence.

Huntington enlisted in the militia as an ensign in 1769, and historian Damien Cregeau notes that he became a full colonel within six years. After the British and the Americans clashed at Concord and Lexington, express

Portrait of Jedidiah Huntington. *Courtesy New York Public Library Digital Collections.*

rider Israel Bissell rode from Massachusetts to Philadelphia with the news. He stopped at Norwich, and Jedidiah Huntington joined Christopher Leffingwell as the first to see the letter announcing the battles.

As commander of the Twentieth Regiment of militia, Huntington mustered his men and headed to Massachusetts. They arrived in Cambridge on April 26 and became part of the twenty thousand troops surrounding Boston, effectively bottling up the British army so it couldn't leave the city by land. British General Thomas Gage began planning to put his troops on heights in Charlestown and Dorchester that overlooked the city and the harbor. By June 15, the provincials were aware of the plans, and the Massachusetts Committee of Safety ordered General Artemus Ward to capture both heights.

For some unknown reason, Colonel William Prescott ordered fortifications built on Breeds Hill rather than the much taller Bunker Hill in Charlestown, and his men worked through the night. When the sun rose, the result of their labor shocked the British, who were greeted by an earthen wall 160 feet long and 30 feet high, according to the Massachusetts Historical Society's online account of the battle. The British ships in the harbor began bombarding the colonials, whose labors continued through the day. By midafternoon, British redcoats were landing in Charlestown and marching up the hill. They attacked twice and were repelled both times by American fire. When they attacked a third time, they overran the exhausted provincials, who had run out of ammunition and resorted to hand-to-hand combat before they retreated. In the end, the British held the hill at the cost of 226 redcoats dead and another 828 wounded. The MHS exhibit put the provincial losses at 140 dead and 271 wounded.

The British general learned that day that the colonists could and would fight and that they could be lethal. It became apparent that the British troops would be in Massachusetts for a longer time than they expected. In fact, the stalemate evolved into a siege of Boston that lasted until the following March. Meanwhile, Congress voted to establish an army, with George Washington as the general in chief. He arrived in June and set about reorganizing the militias into the Continental army.

Back in Norwich, Huntington's wife, Faith, had become depressed, and in his concern for her, Huntington decided to bring her to stay with friends in Dedham, Massachusetts, where he could visit her often and perhaps ease her mind. After he took their son Jabez to Lebanon to live with his grandparents, he and Faith set off for Massachusetts. A problem with the carriage in Providence delayed their arrival in Boston until after the battle. That meant that instead of seeing the excitement of a battle viewed from some distance, they arrived for its aftermath: the putrid odors, the burial details, grief over fallen comrades and wounded men crying out for relief from their pain. A veteran British soldier named Waller described it as "a sight too dreadful for me to dwell on any longer."

Faith saw these horrors of battle, coming face to face with the dangers that threatened her father, brother and husband. She fell into a deep depression, experiencing bouts of "calm tranquility and composure" that would give way to "great and surprising pain and distortion." Wrote her brother John Trumbull, "It overcame her strong but too sensitive mind." For the next five months, Faith apparently alternated between periods of calm and tranquility and increasing agitation that finally led her to hang herself on November 24.

Colonel Huntington's regiment remained near Boston, and they were among the troops atop Dorchester Heights on March 4, 1776. They had probably spent the night of March 3 helping move the Ticonderoga cannons into position overlooking the city and harbor, shocking British troops who awoke to the sight of cannon pointed at them. They remained on post over the next two weeks, until finally, on March 17, they watched as Howe's troops evacuated the city and boarded ships bound for Newfoundland.

General Washington reckoned the next location in British sights would be New York. His troops marched southeast, coming through Norwich as the calendar turned from March to April. As assistant commissary general, Christopher Leffingwell scrambled to feed the troops and their associated animals as they came through town. He was able to find a few head of cattle, and Groton sent up two tons of hay.

Washington himself arrived in Norwich on April 8. It is believed he lunched with Leffingwell at his home, now the Leffingwell House Museum. The general spent the evening at the Huntington Lane home of Jabez Huntington. Originally, Jedidiah Huntington was to entertain Washington, but in the wake of his wife's death, he asked his father to host Washington in his stead. The guest list included Governor Trumbull, who rode in from Lebanon to consult with the general.

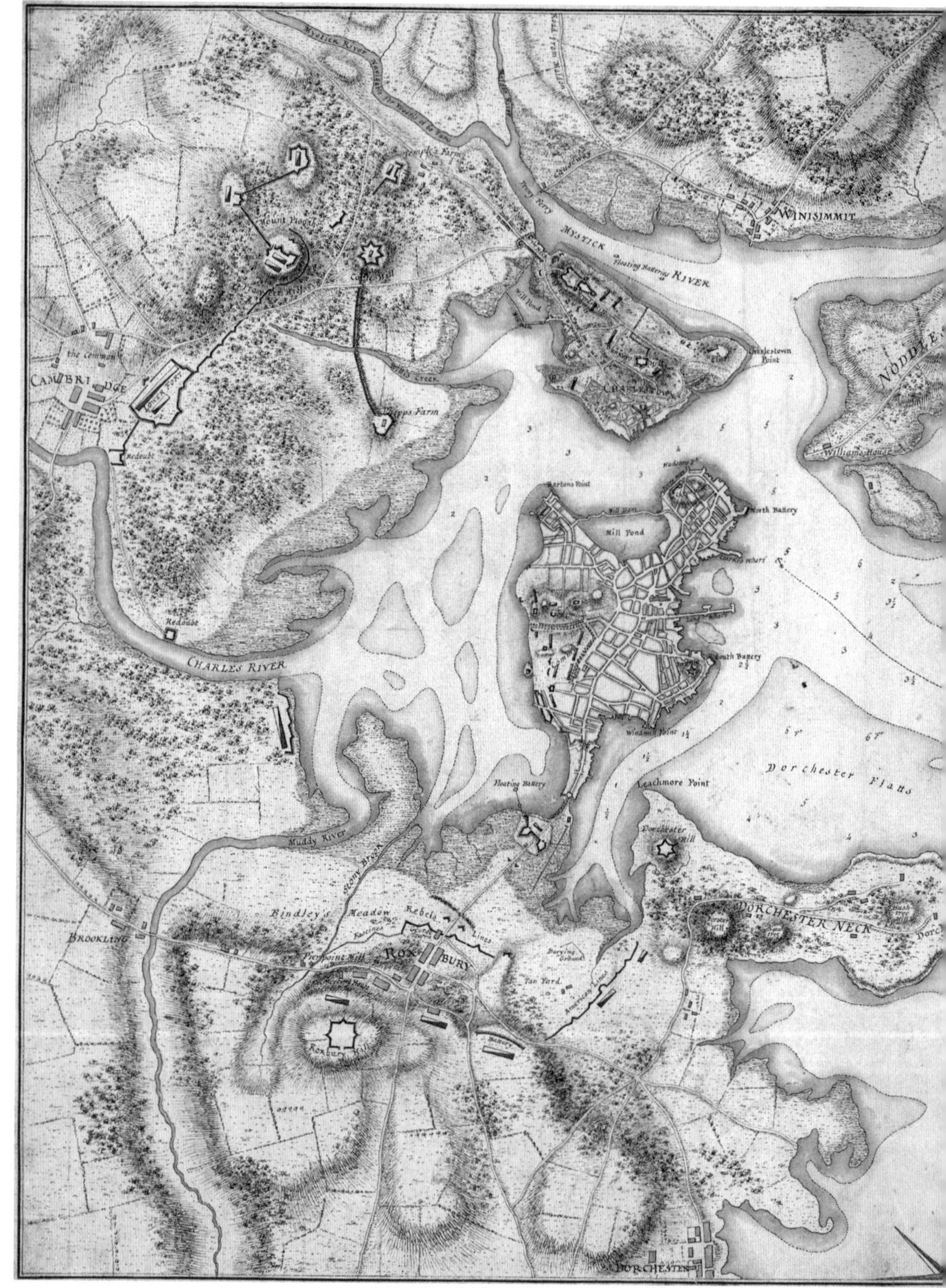
WINISIMMIT
MYSTICK
Floating Battery
RIVER
the Common
Redoubt
Charlestown Point
Williams House
Bartons Point
Mill Dam
Mill Pond
North Battery
South Battery
Windmill Point
CHARLES RIVER
Leachmore Point
Dorchester Flatts
Floating Battery
Muddy River
Stony Brook
Dorchester Hill
DORCHESTER NECK
Bindley's Meadow
Rebels
Lines
ROX BURY
Burying Ground
Tan Yard
American Lines
DORCHESTER

Map depicting the area during the siege of Boston. *Courtesy Library of Congress.*

Huntington's unit, which had become the Seventeenth Continental Regiment, continued to New York and was heavily involved in the Battle of Long Island on August 27, 1776, although without its commanding officer. Huntington had become ill with what may have been malaria and was confined to bed, according to the Society of the Cincinnati account of the battle, which dubbed the regiment Huntington's Heroes. The brutality of the conflict was illustrated as Captain Joseph Jewett of Huntington's regiment surrendered his sword to a British officer, who promptly turned the sword on Jewett. It took two agonizing days for Jewett to die.

The regiment lost 199 men killed or missing. Most of the others were forced into surrendering after a valiant fight against British troops who outnumbered them five to one. In all, 1,000 Americans were captured during that battle, and Huntington's men were about one-quarter of that total. The prisoners of war were loaded onto British ships by surly British captors. The Cincinnati article quotes Lieutenant Jabez Fitch of the Seventeenth Regiment, who described the overcrowded, filthy conditions and inadequate food and water the men endured for the next thirty-nine days.

In October, the men were taken to Manhattan, which was by then occupied by the British. While officers were paroled and permitted to seek quarters with friends or patriot sympathizers in the city, the enlisted men were ordered to churches whose pastors were patriot sympathizers. The British soldiers removed the pews, ordered hundreds of men into each building and then effectively abandoned the prisoners—apparently without any of life's basics, including food, water, heat and sanitation.

Most of Huntington's men were assigned to the Middle Dutch Church at the corner of Nassau and Liberty Streets. The Cincinnati Society article includes a written account by Lieutenant Jonathan Gillette of Huntington's regiment. The lieutenant, who hailed from Lyme, Connecticut, was himself seriously ill with a disease contracted aboard the troopship. Although he apparently was able to visit his men, he was unable to provide any relief for their misery.

> *I will Endeavor to faintly lead you into the poor cituation the soldiers are in, espechally those taken at Long Island where I was; in fact these cases are deplorable and they are Real objects of pitty—they are still confined and in houses where there is no fire—poor mortals, with little or no clothes—perishing with hunger occasioned for want of food—there natures are broke and gone, some almost loose there voices and some there hearing—they are crouded into churches & there guarded night and day. I cant paint the horable*

> *appearance they make—it is shocking to human nature to behold them. Could I draw the curtain from before you; there expose to your view a lean Jawd mortal…his Rotten Rags, close beset with unwelcome vermin. Could I do this, I say,* [it is] *possible I might in some* [small] *manner fix your idea with what appearance sum hundreds of these poor creatures make in houses where once people attempted to Implore God's Blessings, &c, but I must say no more of their calamities. God be merciful to them—I can't afford them no Relief.*

The article describes how the bodies of those who died during the night were carted away each morning and thrown into the empty entrenchments the men had dug a few months earlier. Only about one-third of the captives from Huntington's regiment were still alive by the time a prisoner exchange was arranged in December 1776. The emaciated soldiers were marched to a Lower Manhattan wharf to board a British sloop for what should have been a two-day sail to Connecticut and freedom. It was, instead, eleven days of hell punctuated by an outbreak of smallpox. In all, another twenty-eight men died on the voyage. On January 3, they reached Milford, Connecticut, where the survivors were "unceremoniously dumped ashore" on a brutally cold night. Although the people of Milford tried to help, another forty-six men died there. Any man who managed to reach his home probably brought smallpox with him.

By the following spring, Jedidiah Huntington had recovered enough to be considered for promotion to general, but the promotion was denied by Congress since Connecticut already had its quota of generals. The Connecticut Sons of the American Revolution website includes an April 15, 1777 letter from Colonel Huntington in Norwich to General Washington acknowledging his orders to march to Peekskill, New York, and bemoaning the difficulty of both recruiting and equipping troops.

> *Equiping the Men is attended with the utmost Difficulty, with Blankets in particular—praying & paying hardly prevail with Families to spare from their already exhausted Stores—I shall send on my Men as fast as possible & urge the recruiting Service every Way in my Power….*
>
> *I am, with Affection, Respect & Esteem, Your Excellency's most obedient Servant*
>
> *Jed. Huntington*

Ten days later, Huntington led his First Connecticut Regiment on an overnight trek across Connecticut to provide reinforcements for General

Gold Silliman and fellow Norwich native General Benedict Arnold as they tried to repulse Sir William Tryon's raid on the Danbury supply depot. It was Huntington's troops who harassed the British rear guard all the way back to their ships in Westport. One account compared it to the actions of the patriots in Concord and Lexington who harassed the redcoats as they retreated to Boston.

In the wake of the Battle of Ridgefield, Huntington was promoted to brigadier general on May 12, 1777, and given command of a brigade. With the death of General David Wooster at Ridgefield, Jedidiah's father, Jabez, was promoted to major general and given command of the entire Connecticut militia.

By July, Jedidiah Huntington was at his next post at Peekskill, New York, and his men worked on fortifications across the river from West Point until mid-September, when they rushed to reinforce Washington's troops after his defeat at the Battle of Brandywine. Only his Fifth Connecticut reached Germantown by the October 4 battle there.

General Huntington and his brigade arrived at Valley Forge in December 1777. Recent research by the National Park Service suggests that General Huntington lived in a log cabin, contrary to the long-held belief that he had a stone house (the NPS says the house wasn't built until after the war). Huntington apparently made no secret of his unhappiness at the conditions of limited rations in "this starved country."

Within three months, he was on the move again, dispatched by Washington to investigate circumstances leading to the loss of Forts Montgomery and Clinton along the Hudson River. Huntington was able to visit Norwich in April long enough to marry Ann Moore, the daughter of a loyalist, whom he apparently met while stationed in New York.

A family genealogy describes a scene that occurred a couple months later at West Point but could just as well have applied to Washington's council of war in June 1788. It describes Jedidiah Huntington as "a slightly built man" whose "greatness was rather intellectual and moral than physical."

> *"There is in existence a memorandum of the weighing of several revolutionary officers at West Point, August 19, 1788; when Gen. Washington weighed 209 pounds, Gen. Lincoln, 224, Gen. Knox, 280, and Gen. Huntington, 132," and goes on to quote author Edwin Valentine Mitchell who wrote, "The diminutive General Huntington, weighing only 132…appears like a minnow among the whales."*

Huntington may have been small in stature but apparently had no qualms about speaking up to urge Washington to continue using the caution that had benefited him in the past, even though others were advocating more aggressive action. This time, Washington chose a more aggressive plan.

During the initial exchanges between Continental and British troops at Monmouth, New Jersey, Huntington assisted his Norwich friend Colonel John Durkee, who was wounded in both hands, and then moved his brigade into a position that saw heavy fighting, although accounts of the battle are sparse. A line of cannon had been set up, and later in the afternoon, Dr. William Read observed General Washington riding back and forth along the line when a cannonball landed close enough to throw dirt on the general. He saw John Laurens and Jedidiah Huntington grab the bridle of Washington's horse and urge him to move to a spot where he would be less of a target. The general ignored their advice.

That Washington valued Huntington's judgment is clear, as Huntington was appointed to the court-martial of General Charles Lee for misconduct at the Battle of Monmouth. Huntington had a fairly quiet eighteen months in New York, but September 1780 proved a blockbuster when he learned that a man well known from his boyhood in Norwich, his comrade-in-arms from the siege of Boston and the Battle of Ridgefield, had betrayed the country. General Benedict Arnold, commander at West Point, had plotted with the British to allow them to seize the fort and possibly capture Washington. Arnold had escaped on a British ship, but his British contact, Major John André, had been captured. Once again, Washington turned to Huntington to serve on a court of inquiry, this time into André's behavior as a spy. André was found guilty since he had been a British officer moving about the countryside in civilian clothing and consequently was sentenced to hang.

Huntington's troops and Major Benjamin Tallmadge and his dragoons were sent to the Redding, Connecticut area to deter any British thoughts of attacking Fairfield County in Connecticut during the turmoil over Arnold's treachery. Later that year, Huntington was one of a committee of four who drafted the constitution of the Society of the Cincinnati, a fraternal organization for officers of the war. By December 1780, he commanded the only Connecticut brigade that remained in service. He appears to have spent much of the remainder of the war in the West Point area. In April 1783, Huntington recommended that site for a military academy. At the close of the war, Jedidiah Huntington was breveted a major general.

Others may have profited during the war, but it cost the Huntingtons a great deal. Business suffered not only from state mandates such as

The home of General Jedidiah Huntington in Norwichtown. *Courtesy Leffingwell House Museum/Society of the Founders of Norwich.*

embargoes and duties but also because both Jabez and Jedidiah were often away from home and significant losses were sustained when ships from their fleet were captured or sunk. When the war ended, Jedidiah Huntington returned to Norwich with the hope of resuming the family businesses. With his father's death in 1786, it would be up to him, since his brothers were otherwise occupied.

Jedidiah's brother Andrew (1745–1824), who had been commissary for a brigade during the war, turned to paper manufacturing at the Norwich Falls. Joshua (1751–1821) had commanded a company in Putnam's brigade during the war. In 1777, he had a commission from the Continental Congress to build a thirty-six-gun frigate. Ebenezer (1754–1834), who had left Yale just before graduation to volunteer, stayed in the army until the end of the war, rising to the rank of lieutenant colonel. He was with Washington when the British surrendered at Yorktown. He served as adjutant general of the state's militia for thirty years and served in Congress as representative from Connecticut. In 1798, Ebenezer was commissioned a brigadier general in the U.S. Army during a two-year conflict with France.

Jedidiah continued his government service at both the state and local levels. He became an alderman in Norwich and then state treasurer, member of the Connecticut General Assembly, sheriff of New London County and

Norwich district probate court judge. After the adoption of the Constitution, Huntington was an elector in the nation's first presidential election. In 1789, newly elected President George Washington appointed Huntington collector of revenue for the Port of New London. This lucrative position necessitated a move to New London, where he died in 1818. Historian Cregeau notes that the 1800 New London Harbor lighthouse, the fourth-oldest lighthouse in the United States, is a "lasting emblem of Huntington's legacy."

CHAPTER 5

BENEDICT ARNOLD (1741–1801)

"SOMETIME GENERAL IN GEORGE WASHINGTON'S ARMY"

Benedict Arnold was a war hero and a great patriot—until he wasn't. For nearly 250 years, the name Benedict Arnold has been synonymous with treason. Arnold was the Continental army general who saved the American cause on more than one occasion but also nearly succeeded in delivering a victory to the English foe.

It was Arnold who realized, as the conflict was beginning, that there were cannons for the taking at Fort Ticonderoga in New York. Later, those guns, sited over Boston, prompted the British regulars to withdraw. It was Arnold who led troops on a grueling march across present-day Maine and New Hampshire in brutal winter conditions with the goal of capturing Quebec. It was Arnold who outwitted the British navy at Valcour Island on Lake Champlain. While most of the fleet under his command was destroyed and his losses were twice that of the English, Arnold managed to escape by sailing his remaining ships past the British fleet in the darkness of night and sent General Guy Carleton's army back to Canada for the winter of 1776–77, buying crucial time for the fledgling Continental army. And it was Arnold's strategy and leadership in 1777 that brought an American victory at Saratoga, New York, in a battle that is widely recognized as the turning point of the war for the Americans.

In modern times, Arnold would have been awarded multiple Purple Hearts for the injuries he sustained that cost him the use of his left leg. He was shot and then later shot again and broke the leg in battle when his horse was shot and landed on his leg. Instead, from the beginning, Arnold was dogged by accusations—some lies fabricated by detractors, some more or less true—that included having conflicts of interest, making unethical decisions and overstepping his authority. He used plenty of his own money to provision and outfit his troops, but he was accused of misuse of public funds. When Congress promoted Arnold's former subordinates so that they outranked him, Arnold was given a horse to replace the one that perished in battle.

Benedict Arnold was born in Norwich on January 14, 1741. His family roots stretched back to the early days of the colonies. His father, Benedict Arnold IV, was the grandson of a governor of Rhode Island. The governor owned a large amount of land and considerable wealth, but it had been divided among multiple heirs, leaving Benedict IV apprenticeship to a cooper as his inheritance. Benedict's mother was Hannah Waterman King, the widow of a successful Norwich merchant and sea captain. Her father's family stretched back to the Reverend John Lathrop, who arrived in Boston in 1634. One of her mother's ancestors was Sergeant Thomas Waterman, a founder of Norwich. The Arnold house was located on present-day Washington Street at the corner of Arnold Place. While the house no longer stands, there is a marker to indicate its location.

When Benedict IV and Hannah married in 1733, the senior Benedict took over Absalom King's business and ships and became a successful sea

Benedict Arnold was born in this house in 1741. *Courtesy Library of Congress.*

captain and merchant. They had six children, but their first son, Benedict, died, and then their daughters Mary and Elizabeth and son Absalom died of diphtheria, leaving Benedict V (named to honor his brother) and Hannah the only surviving children. The deaths of his children began a downward spiral for Captain Arnold, who started drinking. As time went on, his finances suffered, the once prominent family was relegated from the front pew to the back of the church and young Benedict was recalled from his school in Plainfield, where he was being prepared to enter college. Several times, the elder Benedict was arrested for public drunkenness. It often fell to young Benedict to go the tavern where his father was drinking to bring him home, a considerable embarrassment for a young man.

As college was no longer possible, young Benedict's mother arranged for him to be apprenticed to some Lathrop cousins who owned the town's apothecary shop at what is now 380 Washington Street. Young Benedict proved successful and progressed from helping in the shop to being a supercargo, responsible for loading their ships, selling the cargo and purchasing and loading cargo for the voyage home. Finally, he captained his own ships, sailing to upstate New York and Canada as well as New York City and the West Indies.

Hannah Arnold died in 1759. After his father died in 1761, young Benedict wanted a fresh start, and with the backing of the Lathrops, he moved to New Haven and set himself up as a druggist and bookseller. His shop was successful, and he became a well-respected businessman. He accepted an invitation to join the Masonic Society, where he met Samuel Mansfield, high sheriff of New Haven County. Benedict Arnold married his daughter Margaret "Peggy" Mansfield on February 22, 1767. Their first son, Benedict, was born the next year, followed by Richard in 1769 and Henry in 1772. Hannah Arnold, Benedict's sister, moved to New Haven at her brother's request and helped Peggy run the shop and care for the Arnolds' sons while Benedict was at sea on one of his three ships.

Engraved portrait of Benedict Arnold. *Courtesy New York Public Library Digital Collections.*

Arnold formed a militia unit that became known as the Second Company, Governors Foot Guard and was elected its captain. The men hired a former British prisoner of war to train them in military drill. In April 1775, when word of the battles at Lexington and

Concord reached New Haven, Arnold mustered his militia to join the fighting. He demanded the keys to the city's powder house so his men could draw gunpowder and ammunition, but the selectmen refused, saying they wanted to wait until they had more information. Arnold was not deterred; he declared that only God would keep him from marching, which prompted the selectmen to relent in the face of his determination.

Arnold and his militia marched to Massachusetts, arriving too late to see any action. On the return trip, Arnold encountered Connecticut's Colonel Samuel Parsons, who bemoaned the Americans' lack of cannon. Thanks to his familiarity with New York and Canada, Arnold realized he knew where cannon could be found at minimal risk and described to Parson the deterioration of Fort Ticonderoga and Crown Point at the southern end of Lake Champlain and the many cannons housed there.

As Arnold returned to Boston, Parsons rode to Hartford and convened a meeting of prominent Connecticut men, including Silas Deane, Samuel Wyllys, Noah Phelps and Christopher Leffingwell. Shortly afterward, Captain Edward Mott arrived from Boston, intending to recruit a company of soldiers who would take the forts, but he was persuaded to accept a commission as supreme commander of the Connecticut troops. The committee borrowed £300 from the colonial treasury and entrusted it to Phelps and Barnard Romance to finance the expedition. Mott, Phelps and Romance set out for Vermont through northwestern Connecticut and southern Berkshire County in western Massachusetts, recruiting as they went.

On their way through Pittsfield, Massachusetts, the Connecticut men were joined by about forty militiamen and two officers who would prove significant in Benedict Arnold's career. One was James Easton, a local tavernkeeper who was described as having a forceful personality but was also "coarse, garrulous and slippery," according to Professor Willard Wallace in his Arnold biography. The other, Professor Wallace says, was Major John Brown, an "energetic, glib-tongued young lawyer," a Yale graduate who had read law with Benedict's cousin Oliver Arnold (the attorney general of Rhode Island) and was married to Oliver's sister.

The militia group arrived in Vermont on May 7 and met with Ethan Allen. They chose Mott to be president of their undertaking and decided Allen should be commander of the troops. Meanwhile, in Boston, Arnold had taken his plan to the Massachusetts Committee of Safety, now the colony's governing body, and obtained a commission and authorization to raise a company of four hundred men to capture the cannon at the New York forts. With £100 in cash, Colonel Arnold headed to western

Massachusetts, where he learned of the Connecticut venture. He then rode hard to the north, arriving at Castleton, Vermont, on May 9. At his first meeting with the Connecticut men and Allen, Arnold imperiously demanded the command for himself, claiming he was the only one with a valid commission. He then confronted Allen, whose men refused to fight under another commander.

By then, it was nearly time to board the boats to cross the lake and commence their attack. Neither Arnold nor Allen was willing to serve under the other's command, but finally, they reluctantly agreed to a joint command. When they landed with the first group of about eighty-five men, the co-commanders approached Fort Ticonderoga and surprised a sentry and the occupants, resulting in a swift surrender with no shots fired on May 10, 1775. They captured more than one hundred thousand pounds of cannon and other armaments, which were transported to Boston by Henry Knox.

The Green Mountain Boys had captured a schooner, but landsmen that they were, they didn't know what to do with it. Arnold, an experienced sailor, took command, renamed the sloop *Liberty*, installed some cannon and then sailed north to St. John on the Richelieu River, just over the Canadian border, where the British moored a seventy-ton warship.

By May 17, Arnold had reached the river, but he was unable to move farther for lack of wind. He and thirty-five men boarded two bateaux and rowed the rest of the way. They surprised the dozen British soldiers at the fort, took them prisoner and seized the warship, some other boats and cannon before returning to Lake Champlain. Arnold's quick action meant the British could not take control of Lake Champlain and the Hudson River until one or more ships were constructed, thus delaying their plan to separate New England from New York and the Southern colonies.

That the English were outraged was to be expected; Arnold did not expect Americans to be upset. Members of the Continental Congress, who were just beginning their session in Philadelphia, had hoped for a peaceful resolution to their differences with England. Arnold's incursion and theft of a warship would make resolution more difficult, maybe even impossible.

Ethan Allen wrote a report for the New York Assembly claiming he took Fort Ticonderoga, adding that Arnold "accompanied" him. His report to Massachusetts ignored Arnold completely while praising Easton and Brown as well as his own Green Mountain Boys. Easton, who hand-delivered the report to the Massachusetts Provincial Congress, had no scruples about denigrating Arnold, especially after Arnold refused to promote him to a colonelcy. And in Connecticut, Edward Mott reported that Arnold's demand to command the force at Ticonderoga nearly resulted in mutiny among the militiamen. Arnold resigned in disgust as Allen became the Hero of Ticonderoga, Easton received his promotion and was given command of Arnold's regiment and Brown was promoted to major in the same regiment, completing their destruction of Arnold.

Despite all the trepidation and thoughts of reconciliation with England, Congress decided to invade Canada in hopes that General George Washington, commander of the newly minted Continental army, could conquer their northern neighbor and perhaps create a fourteenth colony before the English troops arrived in earnest.

Major General Philip Schuyler of New York was tapped to head the invading army rather than Arnold, but that didn't deter Arnold from contacting Schuyler to seek a role in the undertaking. Theirs was a positive meeting, but the discussions were cut short when Arnold received word from New Haven that his wife, Peggy, had died in an epidemic on June 19, 1775, followed by her father three days later. A heavy-hearted Arnold left for home to see his sons and his sister.

EXPEDITION TO QUEBEC, SEPTEMBER 1775

A few weeks later, Arnold had recovered enough to resume pursuit of his military aspirations. This time, he rode to Cambridge to bring General Washington his plan for a two-pronged invasion of Canada. Schuyler would head up Lake Champlain while Arnold would approach from the east, along the Kennebec River through the woods of Maine. They would meet at Quebec to take the city. Washington approved the plan and authorized a force of one thousand soldiers. Arnold chose soldiers from Pennsylvania and Virginia, frontiersmen who could handle themselves in the woods. Arnold ordered construction of a fleet of flat-bottomed boats called bateaux. Two hundred were built in just two weeks; the haste led to the use of inferior materials and shoddy workmanship. When he saw them, an angry Arnold ordered repairs, but he was stuck with boats of green lumber that would warp and split.

Arnold's original maps put the route to Quebec at 180 miles, but the actual distance was 385 miles. Rain, bitter cold and snow created difficult conditions for long portages carrying the heavy bateaux. Leaks spoiled provisions and sank boats. Promised supplies never arrived, reducing the soldiers to eating almost anything, including a broth made by boiling shoe leather. Through it all, the men reported, Arnold seemed to be everywhere, not only offering words of encouragement to them but also actively assisting in the heavy jobs such as carrying the bateaux. One can only imagine their relief when Arnold and a small advance group reached a French settlement whose residents willingly provided provisions for the troops, who hadn't had any rations for five days. The starvation diet, desertions and illnesses such as dysentery and smallpox reduced their numbers to about six hundred emaciated, weakened men by the time they approached Quebec.

Two British warships anchored in the river led to the realization that Arnold had been betrayed by an Indian who was supposed to deliver a message to a friend of Arnold's in Quebec. Instead, he brought the message to a British officer, enabling the British to set up patrols along the St. Lawrence River and destroy or seize all the small boats along the river, leaving Arnold and his men without a way to cross.

November came without word from Schuyler's army, which was supposed to be meeting Arnold's. Finally, Arnold learned they had been delayed by a six-week siege at St. John and that Schuyler, who had become ill and returned home, had been replaced by Brigadier General Richard Montgomery. Once Montgomery arrived on December 2, events moved quickly, and the Americans began a monthlong siege of Quebec. On December 31, despite a blizzard, they attacked, but the snow hampered visibility and clogged gun barrels. At the end of the fighting, Montgomery had been killed, Arnold had been wounded by a bullet in the thigh and four hundred men had been captured. After continuing the siege for several more months, Arnold withdrew when spring came.

Although Arnold was hailed as a hero and dubbed "America's Hannibal," Congress sent a committee headed by Benjamin Franklin to discover why the Quebec campaign failed. The committee praised Arnold, as did the British. General Washington declared that Arnold had great merit, and Congress promoted Arnold to major general.

And then came James Easton and John Brown, who had been reprimanded by Arnold for misuse of private property at Crown Point. They went to Philadelphia to lay charges against Arnold. Brown accused Arnold of "pillaging" throughout Canada, promising that proof was forthcoming. Lacking a response from Arnold, who was more than two hundred miles away at Fort Ticonderoga, some of the members of the Congress accepted Brown's report as true. Apparently, they figured where there's smoke, there's fire.

In the end, nothing came of Arnold's reprimands against Brown and Easton, both of whom were promoted with a year's back pay. Their charges against Arnold remained for a while but eventually were dropped. General Horatio Gates, the new commander in the north, assigned Arnold a new command: defense of Lake Champlain.

According to historian David King, Arnold wrote to Gates, "I cannot but think it extremely cruel, when I have sacrificed my ease, health and a great part of my private property in the cause of my country to be [vilified] as a robber and thief—at a time, too, when I have it not in my power to be heard in my own defense." He and other historians suggest that Arnold's zeal to accomplish his objectives caused him to ignore such mundane things as accurate recordkeeping. Apparently, Arnold would use his own funds to provide for his men but often neglected to keep receipts, records and bills to document how money was being spent.

Author Nathaniel Philbrick, in an interview, described Arnold thus:

> *Abrupt and impatient with anything he deemed superfluous to the matter at hand, Arnold had a fatal tendency to criticize and even ridicule those with whom he disagreed.*
>
> *When a few weeks later a Continental Army officer named James Easton dared to question the legitimacy of his authority as the self-proclaimed commodore of the American Navy on Lake Champlain, Arnold proceeded to "kick him very heartily."*
>
> *It was an insult Easton never forgot, and in the years ahead, he became one of a virtual Greek chorus of Arnold detractors who would plague him for the rest of his military career.*
>
> *And yet, if a soldier served with him during one of his more heroic adventures, that soldier was likely to regard him* [Arnold] *as the most inspiring officer he had ever known.*

Valcour Island, New York, October 11, 1776

As British ships headed to Lake Champlain, Arnold took his fleet north to Valcour Island and anchored in a bay on the northern end of the island. A day of fighting left the Americans with only a few boats, which were effectively bottled up in the bay as a line of British ships anchored across the entrance. Arnold realized he couldn't fight his way out, but after darkness fell that moonless night, he ordered his men to row the boats past the British, using fog for cover as they headed to Crown Point. The next morning, an angry British General Carleton sent his ships after the Americans. As they fought over the next two days, many of the American boats were purposely run aground and destroyed so the British couldn't capture them. Arnold himself put the torch to his flagship before marching overland to Crown Point with his remaining two hundred men.

As it turned out, four of Arnold's ships had escaped the British, but nevertheless, it was clear that Lake Champlain was in British control. After destroying the fort at Crown Point, Arnold and his troops headed back to Fort Ticonderoga. For his part, Carleton recognized the onset of winter and took his troops to winter quarters, abandoning any additional effort to move into the Hudson River Valley.

Once again, Arnold had delayed British movement to the Americans' advantage. Still, there was General David Waterbury claiming Arnold saved himself at the expense of the other ship captains. Waterbury's ship was run aground and he himself was captured. He included his accusations in his after-action report, and again, delegates to the Congress believed they had proof of Arnold's wrongdoing.

In 1777, the British devised a strategy that would separate rebellious New England from the other colonies, which were presumably less eager for independence. They planned a pincer movement in which from the west, General Barry St. Leger in Ontario would move into New York along the Mohawk River. From the south, troops commanded by General William Howe would move north from New York City through the Hudson River Valley, while General John Burgoyne came south from Montreal. The three would converge near Albany, New York.

Fort Stanwix, August 1777

General St. Leger progressed far enough to lay siege to Fort Stanwix, located near present-day Rome, New York, with an army that included a large number of Native Americans. After three weeks, American troops commanded by General Nicholas Herkimer were ambushed on their way to relieve the soldiers in the fort. Their encounter on August 6 became known as the Battle of Oriskany, one of the bloodiest of the war, leaving nearly five hundred Americans killed, wounded or captured. They included General Herkimer, who was wounded in the leg and died after a failed amputation.

Benedict Arnold and a force of nine hundred were ordered to relieve the troops at Fort Stanwix. Hoping to avoid a battle with a much larger force, Arnold offered a prisoner the opportunity to avoid a death sentence if he would persuade the enemy that Arnold had a huge number of soldiers. During the Quebec campaign, Arnold had been dubbed Dark Eagle by one of the Indian guides. The prisoner, who was considered a sort of prophet by the tribesmen, persuaded St. Leger's Native warriors that Dark Eagle was coming with soldiers as numerous as the leaves on the trees. The Indians withdrew, leaving St. Leger with a seriously depleted force, prompting him to retreat as well.

Burgoyne moved his soldiers out of Montreal in early June. He was victorious at Fort Ticonderoga in July but lost nearly one thousand men in an August 16 battle at Bennington, Vermont. Most of his Indigenous fighters left, further reducing the size of his army. By now, it was mid-September, and Burgoyne was left with the choice to take his troops to winter quarters or continue toward Albany. He decided to continue toward Albany, crossed the Hudson River and then camped just north of Saratoga. For his part, Howe never headed north; instead, he went to Philadelphia.

BATTLE OF SARATOGA, FREEMAN'S FARM, SEPTEMBER 19, 1777

The Americans were camped at Stillwater, just south of Saratoga. General Horatio Gates was assigned to replace Schuyler, whom he disliked, as commanding officer. This meant Arnold would be serving under a rival who had wanted for himself a prestigious command that had earlier been given to Arnold. When Arnold chose as his staff officers connected to Schuyler, it fueled Gates's antagonism. Large number of recruits were joining the American army in response to the brutal murder of a White woman by Native warriors under Burgoyne's command. The British commander had no similar way to increase his numbers.

On September 19, Gates moved the American army to high ground at Bemis Heights, overlooking a farm that had been owned by loyalist John Freeman before he moved his family to Canada. According to the National Park Service, Freeman returned to Saratoga as a soldier in one of Burgoyne's regiments.

Gates set his soldiers to building breastworks under the direction of Polish engineer Thaddeus Kosciusko. They spotted Burgoyne's army crossing the

Hudson River a few miles to the north. Gates believed they could fight from behind the breastworks, while Arnold advocated for positioning men in the woods surrounding the field, to prevent the British from flanking the American army.

Although the Americans outnumbered the British by more than two to one, control of the field went back and forth all afternoon, but at the end of the day, Burgoyne's troops dominated. Gates refused Arnold's requests for more troops to repel the British until late in the day, but by then, he had recalled Arnold, leaving the additional troops nowhere to go.

Historians have differed over Arnold's role in the battle: Was he actively leading and encouraging the troops, or did he remain behind the lines, directing troop movements while Gates sat in his tent? Field commanders and the men gave Arnold much of the credit for a fight that left the British with twice as many casualties as the Americans. Since many of the troops involved in the battle were Arnold's, and Gates had little actual battlefield experience, it seems likely Arnold would have been directly involved. Yet it would have been foolhardy for any general to be out on the front lines during a battle.

General Gates prepared for Congress and Governor Clinton of New York a report on the battle that omitted Arnold's role in it. When Arnold objected, observers said, there was a shouting match. When Arnold demanded a transfer to Washington's army, Gates gave Arnold's command to Benjamin Lincoln. Arnold didn't leave camp, and Gates continued ignoring him.

Battle of Saratoga, Bemis Heights, October 7, 1777

Over the next couple of weeks, the armies skirmished, and British General Sir Henry Clinton came up from New York City. His troops captured three forts, but Clinton was little help to Burgoyne as he attacked Bemis Heights, sustaining casualties of one hundred British soldiers killed, wounded or captured. Although Arnold had been ordered to stand down for the duration and was supposed to be in his tent, he suddenly appeared on the battlefield, agitated enough that some observers thought him drunk. He immediately joined the fray, exhorting soldiers, redirecting them to take advantage of weaknesses in the British lines and racing back and forth along the battle line, heedless of bullets and cannonballs flying all around him.

Arnold was shot in the leg that had been wounded at Quebec. Then the horse he was riding was shot, and when it fell, Arnold's wounded leg was crushed beneath it, causing further damage to the broken bone. Arnold was quoted as saying he wished he had been shot in the heart, because had he died in the battle, he would have been famed as a heroic martyr. Burgoyne recognized his defeat and retreated to nearby Schuylerville, which he held before the battle. A week later, he surrendered.

In Gates's report to Congress, he all but ignored Arnold. He mentioned a considerable number of American wounded, continuing, "Amongst the latter is the gallant Major Gen Arnold whose Leg was fractured by a Musket Ball as he was forcing the heavy's Breach Work." Then Gates immediately continued, "Too much Praise cannot be given" to the corps commanded by Colonel Morgan. Gates was credited with a great victory and given command of the army in the south. Arnold's contribution was recognized by restoration of his seniority.

After the battle, Arnold was bedridden for the next five months, having narrowly avoided amputation of his leg. This apparently allowed him plenty

I Benedict Arnold Major General do acknowledge the UNITED STATES of AMERICA to be Free, Independent and Sovereign States, and declare that the people thereof owe no allegiance or obedience to George the Third, King of Great-Britain; and I renounce, refuſe and abjure any allegiance or obedience to him; and I do Swear that I will, to the utmoſt of my power, ſupport, maintain and defend the ſaid United States againſt the ſaid King George the Third, his heirs and ſucceſſors, and his or their abettors, aſſiſtants and adherents, and will ſerve the ſaid United States in the office of Major General which I now hold, with fidelity, according to the beſt of my ſkill and underſtanding.

Sworn before me this 30th. May 1778 – at the Artillery Park Valley Forge H Knox B

B Arnold

Benedict Arnold declared his loyalty to the United States of America on May 30, 1778. *Courtesy Library of Congress.*

of time to consider his future with the Americans and begin to contemplate joining the British.

Although Gates ignored Arnold's role in the victory, a monument to Arnold was erected at the Saratoga battlefield. John Watts de Peyster, an officer of the Saratoga Monument Association, had it erected in 1887 "in memory of the 'most brilliant soldier' of the Continental Army who was desperately wounded on this spot." Because of Arnold's later treason, it shows nothing about Arnold personally, not even his name. Rather, the image depicts an empty boot with a general's epaulets on top.

After the Battle of Saratoga

Saratoga in 1777 was a turning point in the war. It became clear that the Americans could, and would, fight hard and that they could defeat the British. That, in turn encouraged France, which committed to supporting the patriot cause with men, financial aid (cash, donations, loans), armament and supplies.

For the next year, Arnold convalesced. On May 30, 1778, he was at Valley Forge, where he signed the Loyalty Oath, in which he swore he would "to the utmost of my power, support, maintain and defend the said United States against the said King George the Third…and will serve the said United States in the office of Major General which I now hold, with fidelity to the best of my skill and understanding."

After the British left Philadelphia in 1778, Arnold was made military governor of the city. It didn't take long before he was fighting with Congress as well as the governments of Pennsylvania and Philadelphia. There were allegations that Arnold used military transport for personal business. The saving grace for Arnold during his time in Philadelphia was probably making the acquaintance of Margaret "Peggy" Shippen, daughter of a prominent judge with loyalist leanings. Although he was twenty years older than Peggy, Arnold was totally smitten with the young beauty. It should have been a somewhat awkward situation for the military governor, not only because of the optics of his interest in an eighteen-year-old girl but also because British officers had been frequent visitors at the Shippen residence. Among them was Major John André, who was an aide to General Henry Clinton and a British intelligence officer. Arnold married Peggy Shippen on April 8, 1779. Although nobody knows for sure, it seems probable that by then, Arnold was seriously considering defecting to the British, and it's considered likely that Peggy gave him the final push he needed.

In furtherance of the plot, Arnold persuaded General Washington to make him commander of the American fort on the Hudson River at West Point, New York. Arnold began sending information to General Sir Henry Clinton in New York, working through André. Peggy was still corresponding with Major André, and there are letters written by one of Peggy's cousins to André with messages from Peggy in invisible ink between the lines.

On September 20, 1780, the British ship *Vulture* brought André up the Hudson to meet Arnold at the home of loyalist Joshua Hett Smith near West Point. Arnold was to make it easy for the British to capture West Point; in turn, the British would pay him £20,000, estimated to be $6 million today, and a military command. The meeting ran long, and the *Vulture* moved away under American gunfire. André was persuaded that the only way he could return to Clinton in New York was to ride back wearing civilian clothing. A trio of militiamen intercepted him, and while searching André, they found in his boot both a pass written by General Arnold and the plans for West Point. They brought him to their commander, who sent the papers to Washington, who happened to be on his way to confer with Arnold at West Point.

As commandant of West Point, Arnold was also notified about the discovery (since his status as a spy was then unconfirmed). He immediately returned home, spoke with his wife and left aboard the *Vulture*, which had sailed back upriver. When Washington arrived, Peggy appeared hysterical and demanded to know what Washington had done with her husband, ultimately persuading all observers of her innocence. Arnold wrote to Washington, seeking safety for his wife and assuring Washington she had no knowledge of the affair. Peggy was permitted to return to her father's house and then to go to New York, which was still under British control.

André, meanwhile, was tried as a spy, since he had been a military officer dressed in civilian clothing when he was apprehended. Although he asked for a firing squad as befitting an officer, the twenty-eight-year-old André was hanged on October 2, 1780. His death was mourned by British and Americans alike, many of whom blamed Arnold for the death of a popular young officer. People in Norwich were so angered by Arnold's perfidy that they destroyed both Benedict Arnold headstones in the Colonial Burying Ground—his father's and his elder brother Benedict's. His mother's stone was left untouched, as the consensus in town was that Hannah Arnold was a saint. A popular myth in Norwich has it that General Arnold returns each October 31 to weep at his mother's grave. A local film production

On Board the Vulture Sepr 25th
1780

Sir

The Heart which is Conscious of its own rectitude, Cannot attempt to palliate a Step, which the world may Censure as wrong; I have ever acted from a Principle of Love to my Country, since the Commencement of the present unhappy Contest between Great Britain and the Colonies, the same principle of Love to my Country Actuates my present Conduct, however it may appear Inconsistent to the World: who very Seldom Judge right of any Mans Actions.

I have no favor to ask for myself. I have too often experienced the

1030

The first page of Arnold's letter to George Washington seeking safe passage and mercy for his wife, Peggy, after his defection. *Courtesy Library of Congress.*

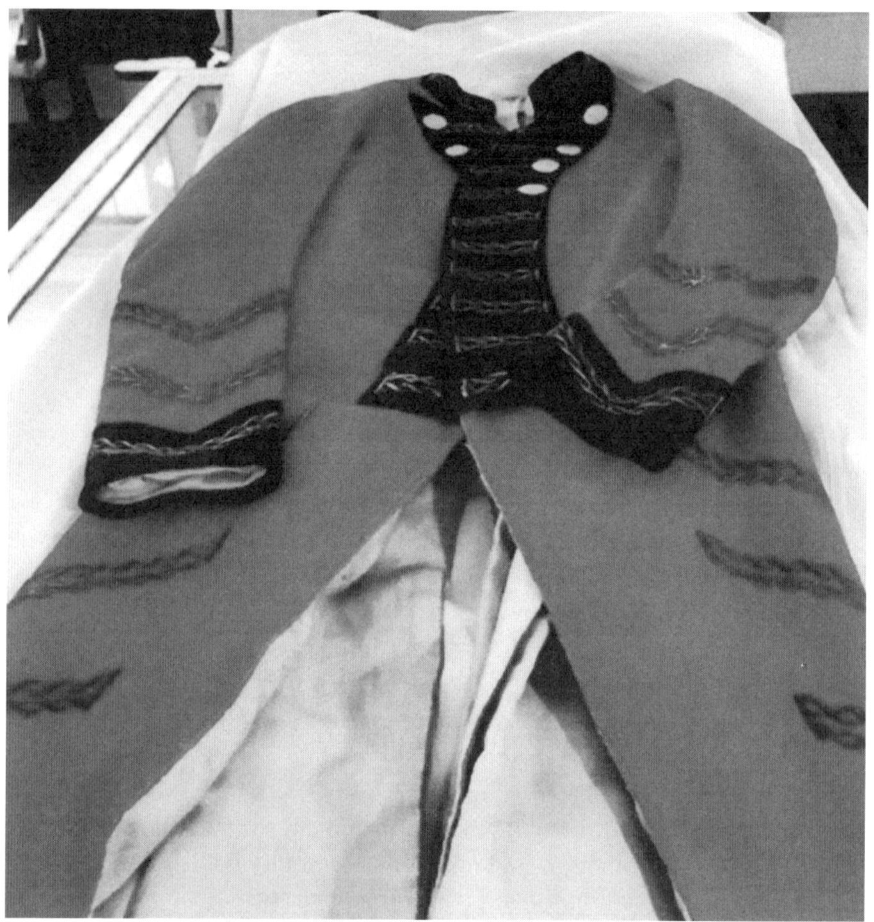

Benedict Arnold wore this uniform, now owned by a Canadian descendant. *Photo by the author.*

depicting a fictious trial of Arnold opens with Arnold kneeling at his mother's grave.

As a British officer, Arnold wasn't entirely trusted, but he was eventually allowed to lead raids in Virginia and, on September 6, 1781, another about twelve miles south of Norwich at the mouth of the Thames River. His men stormed Fort Griswold on the Groton side of the river; British losses were so severe that the British survivors turned the fight into a massacre. The American commanding officer, Colonel William Ledyard, was fatally stabbed with his own sword as he attempted to surrender. Many other Americans were bayonetted. Across the river in New London, Arnold ordered the ships at the wharves burned. It's uncertain how, but the fire spread to residences, destroying much of New London and some of Groton as well.

The Arnolds left for Britain in December 1781. Their welcome wasn't quite an enthusiastic as they anticipated, although King George pronounced himself charmed by Peggy and gave her an annual pension of £500 for the services she had rendered. Arnold began seeking his payment from Clinton barely two weeks after André's death, according to Professor Wallace. Since West Point was never delivered, Clinton reduced the payment to £6,000, with an additional $350 for expenses. Arnold also was given a colonel's commission in the cavalry at £450 annually, with half that as a pension for the rest of his life. He also was made a brigadier general in the Provincial army at £200 more annually until the war's end. Furthermore, Arnold was granted 13,400 acres of land in Canada, where Crown land was reserved for loyalists, Wallace noted.

Arnold's sons with Margaret Mansfield were given army commissions with lifelong half pay. Arnold's children with Peggy Shippen each received a £100 annual pension. All told, for many years, the king was paying the Arnolds more than £1,400 annually in pensions for a plot that never came to fruition.

Arnold set up a merchant shipping business in New Brunswick, Canada, and eventually Peggy and the children joined him. Hannah and the older children came from New Haven, and Hannah remained in Canada with Richard and Henry when Benedict and Peggy returned to England after their hopes for New Brunswick failed to materialize.

Life wasn't much better in England: Arnold lost his business, his son Benedict died while in military service in Jamaica and Arnold fought a duel with the Earl of Lauderdale in response to an insult. Arnold was denied a military assignment each time he asked. His daughter Sophia had a stroke, and Peggy became a semi-invalid, while Arnold himself still suffered from the aftereffects of his leg wounds, gout and asthma.

Arnold fell victim to a fever in 1801 and died on June 12. Peggy died of cancer three years later. They were buried in a crypt in St. Mary's Church in the London neighborhood of Battersea on the banks of the Thames River, unremarked for many years.

The late Bill Stanley of Norwich was for many years an Arnold advocate. He boasted of being suspended from high school for writing a paper that identified Arnold as the greatest American, citing his role in the battle at Saratoga as the turning point of the war. In his later life, Stanley became an Arnold historian and visited all the important sites of Arnold's life. In

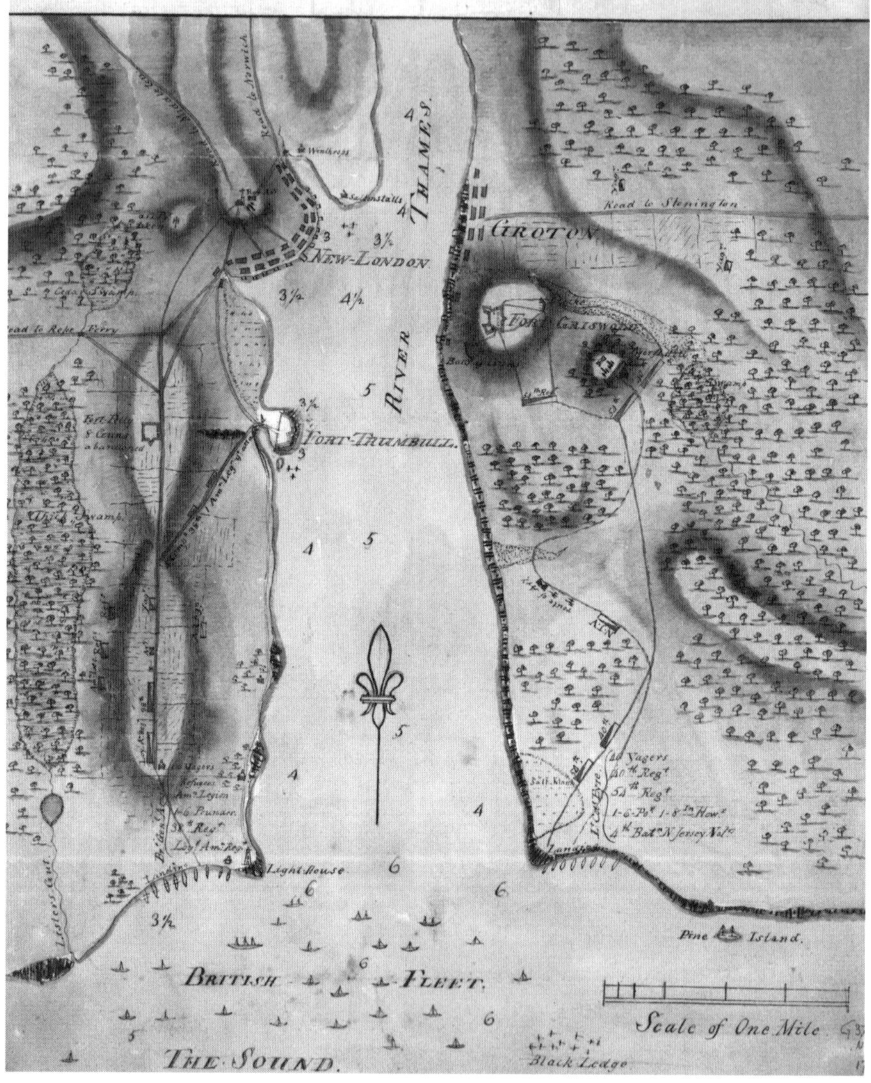

British soldiers commanded by Benedict Arnold attacked Fort Griswold (also known as Groton Heights) and New London on September 6, 1781. *Courtesy the National Archives and Records Administration.*

London, it troubled him that Arnold's burial site was almost unmarked in a room that the church used as a kindergarten. Stanley, a former Connecticut state senator, arranged for a proper marker to be affixed to the crypt. In an interview, Stanley explained why he raised the money to buy the marker, asking, "If we can forgive the Japanese for Pearl Harbor, why can't we forgive him?"

The inscription Stanley placed on the marker reads, "Sometime general in the army of George Washington....The two nations whom he served in turn in the years of their enmity have united in enduring friendship."

Chapter 6

SAMUEL HUNTINGTON (1731–1796)

"A Sensible, Candid and Worthy Man"

As a signer of the Declaration of Independence, Samuel Huntington pledged his life, fortune and sacred honor to the cause of independence, and he made good on that promise. He wasn't a soldier, but with his pen he fought for independence as surely as his cousins and neighbors who joined the army. Huntington knew the law and he knew how to apply the law, and for fifty years, he used his knowledge and skills to benefit his town, his colony and state and his nation.

When Samuel was born on July 16, 1731, he was part of an illustrious family. His great-grandfather Simon Huntington was one of the thirty-nine founders of Norwich. His grandfather Joseph Huntington was one of the founders of Windham, and his father, Nathaniel, had a role in establishing Scotland as an entity separate from the Town of Windham. Another great-grandfather, Matthew Marvin, was an early colonist, coming to the new world in 1635 and settling in Hartford in 1638.

Samuel's parents, Nathaniel and Mehetabel (Thurston) Huntington, had ten children; he was the second son and fourth child. They lived in a two-story house on 180 acres near Merrick's Brook, in what was called Scotland Parish in Windham, now the town of Scotland, Connecticut. Nathaniel Huntington was a farmer and clothier. Although not wealthy like some of the other Huntingtons, he was considered well-to-do and was successful enough to send three sons to Yale. Some biographies suggest Samuel's origins were impoverished and that he was apprenticed to a cooper, but others note there is no record of any apprenticeship agreement or mention of an apprenticeship in letters or contemporary documents. It is more likely, especially with his older brother away at school, that Samuel worked the farm with his father.

Samuel likely attended the local common school. Larry R. Gerlach, author of the 1976 biography *Connecticut Congressman: Samuel Huntington 1731–1796*, notes that, as evidenced by the writings of his later years, Samuel's spelling, punctuation and syntax were "irregular." It appears he had a love of learning and reading, however, as he obtained use of the library of the Reverend Ebenezer Devotion, the first pastor at the new church in Scotland Parish. He would have pored over law books with local lawyers, and in 1754, Samuel Huntington was given leave to practice law in Connecticut.

Over the next five years, Samuel's law practice grew as he took the cases that came his way, but apparently, the new lawyer was overshadowed by the town's older, more experienced attorneys and found it difficult to increase his caseload. In 1760, Samuel Huntington moved to Norwich and hung out his shingle in the larger town that promised more opportunities for an ambitious young man.

In the early years, Windham and Norwich were similar agricultural communities. By the mid-eighteenth century, Norwich's location at the confluence of three rivers had positioned it to become both a trade and manufacturing center. It also didn't hurt that the Huntingtons were a prominent family with many connections who might be inclined to welcome a cousin. Gerlach reports that initially, Huntington's law practice was routine legal work, such as wills and estates, real estate transactions and collection of debts. Within ten years, his clientele was no longer limited to eastern Connecticut. Norwich had moved beyond its agricultural roots and developed into a busy seaport town with a substantial amount of trade, both in the Norwich area and in ports along the eastern coast as far south as Charleston, South Carolina, as well Boston and New York. Norwich ships visited the West Indies and sometimes England and France. Besides the basics, legal work in Norwich would have addressed questions of partnerships, contracts and insurance.

Samuel may also have wanted to increase his income so he could support a wife. On April 17, 1761, in Windham, he married the Reverend Devotion's daughter Martha and brought her to Norwich to live, first on what is now New London Turnpike and later in the mansion he built at 34 East Town Street, which is now the headquarters of United Community and Family Services.

Martha's mother was Martha Lathrop, which brought additional Norwich connections through her family. Her great-great-grandfather Samuel Lathrop and his wife came to Norwich around 1668 and produced many Lathrop descendants. Although the Samuel Huntingtons never had children, they raised a niece and nephew as their own. Samuel (1765–1817) and Frances (1769–1837) Huntington were the children of the senior Samuel's brother Joseph Huntington and Martha's sister Hannah Devotion Huntington, who died at age twenty-six in 1771. Joseph and Hannah's third child, Joseph Huntington Jr. (1767–1794), remained in Coventry with his father and his second wife, who together had nine children. Joseph Huntington was the elder Huntington brother who went to Yale and became a minister.

Samuel Huntington, signer of the Declaration of Independence. *Courtesy the New York Public Library Digital Collection.*

Sammy and Fanny, as the children were known, remained with their aunt and uncle in Norwich even after their father remarried. Caulkins described a happy household where some kind of lively entertainment was always afoot. As an adult, Fanny married the Reverend Edward D. Griffin, who became president of Williams College in Massachusetts. Young Samuel attended Yale in 1785 and then became a lawyer. After his uncle's death, he moved to Ohio and settled in what is now known as the Western Reserve working as a land agent and hotelkeeper. He served on the state's Supreme Court and later became Ohio's third governor.

A third child, Mason Fitch Cogswell, stayed with the Huntingtons after his mother died when he was eleven. His father was the Reverend James Cogswell, successor to Martha's father at the Scotland church. Mason's mother was the daughter of Colonel Jabez Fitch, whose diary gave an account of his time at Forts Edward and Ticonderoga with Major John Durkee during the French and Indian War. About a year after his mother died, his father married Martha Lathrop Devotion, Martha Huntington's widowed mother, making Mason her stepbrother.

After a few years with the Huntingtons, Mason Cogswell left for Yale, where he was valedictorian of his class. After graduation, he studied medicine and became a well-known physician and surgeon, among the first to perform cataract surgery. He became interested in education for the deaf when his daughter Alice lost her hearing at age two. Cogswell was one of the founders of the American School for the Deaf in Hartford.

Lawyers seem to gravitate to politics, and Samuel Huntington was no exception. He became involved in town politics and became the town's tax collector, a justice of the peace and moderator of the Norwich Town Meeting. As the town's attorney, Huntington argued cases that involved everything from opposing highway construction, settling boundary lines and collection from tax delinquents to petitioning the Connecticut General Assembly. Of particular note was an application for Norwich residents to obtain land west of the Susquehanna purchase. Expansion of the Connecticut colony into lands claimed in Pennsylvania was a hot political topic throughout the state. Speculators who invested in the Susquehanna or Delaware Companies were, of course, hoping to make good on their investment. Residents of Pennsylvania regarded the arrival of the settlers from Connecticut as an incursion.

Joan Nafie's *To the Beat of a Drum*, suggests that Connecticut's vehement response to the new British laws originated with the Royal Proclamation of 1763 that banned expansion of the colonies into western lands, which included the land claimed for the Susquehanna and Delaware settlements. Many of eastern Connecticut's most prominent residents had invested in development companies, apparently seeking to become landholders in an era when owning land demonstrated one's wealth. It's not altogether clear that Samuel Huntington Esq. was himself an investor, since he had been a young lawyer with limited income as the companies were being formed. The Samuel Huntington on the company's rolls is more likely a cousin who lived in nearby Canterbury, but Samuel Esq. may have taken some shares at a later date.

Loss of that land would leave many investors/speculators in eastern Connecticut with worthless shares in the Delaware and Susquehanna Companies. This became one of the issues dominating Connecticut politics, and such was the political climate Huntington entered when he was first elected to the Connecticut General Assembly, the legislature's lower house, in 1764.

By 1770, the state legislature was dominated by members who supported Connecticut's venture into Pennsylvania. Gerlach describes Norwich as "an economically progressive yet socially conservative community," for which Huntington was well suited. The conservative Huntington was reelected yearly for the next ten years. Serving in the legislature brought Samuel into contact with men from all over the state and brought him to the attention of Governor Jonathan Trumbull.

In 1765, Governor Johnathan Trumbull appointed Samuel Huntington king's attorney—in essence the district attorney—for the colony of Connecticut. Ten years later, he was named a superior court judge, an appointment that carried with it a seat on the Connecticut Governor's Council. In 1774, Huntington was named to the Connecticut Supreme Court. At that time, judges rode circuit, which meant court convened in locations around the state. For Samuel Huntington, this meant exposure to still more people of varying social and economic classes.

As the English Parliament imposed ever more punitive measures on the colonies, Huntington spoke out, notably against the Coercive Acts of 1774, which became more commonly known as the Intolerable Acts. These laws passed by the British parliament closed the Port of Boston, revoked the Massachusetts charter, moved trials of British officials to England and authorized colonial governors to quarter troops in private homes. Until 1774, Huntington had remained moderate, likely a reflection of his position as attorney for the town and the king, but the colonial reaction to the new acts was an excellent characterization: they were intolerable.

The punitive measures against Boston had ripple effects that reached Norwich. When people from Boston began leaving to escape the British occupation of the city, some came to Norwich. Perhaps they had family or business ties to the town; perhaps it was where the stagecoaches stopped. A town meeting was called on March 28 to address what the town should do about accepting refugees from Boston. How, the question was posed, can we be sure the refugees are patriots and not British spies?

Samuel Huntington, two doctors, three merchants, a real estate speculator and a farmer were appointed to a committee to answer that question. Half an hour later, they recommend not allowing into the town anyone who supported Massachusetts Governor Thomas Hutchinson unless they had a certificate from the Provincial Congress. Furthermore, they recommended, the selectmen or the committee must ensure that refugees understood the town's position: that is, Norwich was a patriot town, and loyalists weren't welcome. The town meeting voted to defend the town and cooperate with other colonies to that end.

Huntington was appointed to Governor Trumbull's Council of Safety, and in October 1775, the General Assembly elected Samuel Huntington one of Connecticut's delegates to the Second Continental Congress. In January 1776, Huntington and Oliver Wolcott departed on a two-week trip to Philadelphia. A biography published by the Connecticut State Library notes that Huntington was almost immediately felled by smallpox and couldn't assume his duties in Congress until February.

The next four months were filled with long days, and perhaps nights, of committee meetings and what must have seemed like endless discussion.

Huntington found he missed his family, and he worried about finances, as he was not in Norwich to do legal work for which he would be paid and his salary from Congress was not enough to meet his expenses—if it was paid at all.

As a member of the Committee on the Manufacture of Arms, Huntington contacted Elijah Backus with the offer of a contract for his Norwich ironworks to produce two thousand guns with bayonets at a price of twelve dollars apiece.

By June, the delegates were enduring the discomfort of hot weather in the city, and Huntington was probably longing for the relatively cool breezes of relatively rural Norwichtown, but there was work to be done. Connecticut's delegates were finally notified that the General Assembly had authorized them to vote for independence, enabling the Connecticut delegation, including Samuel Huntington, to vote aye on July 4, 1776. Five days later, on July 9, the self-educated Connecticut lawyer added his name to the signers of the Declaration of Independence.

A long ten months after arriving in Philadelphia, Huntington went back to Norwich and apparently was immediately drawn into the local aspects of the war: obtaining provisions, dealing with inflation, persuading men to enlist in the militia and protecting the coast—and, by extension, Norwich.

Since the Thames was a navigable river, it was reasonable to think that the British might sail north to Norwich. In the meantime, the provincials used Norwich as a port for captured prize ships. In addition, captured prisoners of war and Tories were sent to Norwich for confinement. Caulkins identified the most notorious prisoner early in the war as Dr. Benjamin Church, a prominent and trusted member of Boston's Sons of Liberty and effectively chief surgeon of Washington's army, until it was discovered he had been selling information to British General Thomas Gage for several years.

Rather than returning to Philadelphia in 1777, Huntington opted to remain in Norwich to help deal with problems closer to home. He represented Connecticut at a meeting of representatives from New England states and New York to discuss the ever-present economic issues of inflation, paper money and prices. Of great urgency was a shortage of salt, a necessity of the time to preserve food. The experience gave Huntington the states' perspective on war-related issues when he returned to Congress in 1778. He arrived to find that the new Articles of Confederation had been written in his absence. Although he thought the document imperfect, Huntington recognized the need for some kind of unified government and supported its passage.

A year later, Huntington returned to Philadelphia, where his committee assignments included creating a plan for negotiating peace with England and devising a system for courts of appeal. Besides conduct of the war, military pay and the ever-present currency problems demanded a large share of delegates' attention.

By September, Huntington was ready to return to his home, but John Jay, the president of Congress, had been appointed minister to Spain. The delegates turned to Huntington as president. He had seniority and experience and a reputation as a cool, rational thinker who apparently didn't feel bound to put regional interests over those of the nation as a whole. Delegate Benjamin Rush of Pennsylvania characterized Huntington as "a sensible, candid and worthy man, and wholly free from State prejudices."

The president of the Continental Congress may not have had a great deal of direct power, but through his leadership, he could influence whether the delegates could merge their differing viewpoints into compromises that would allow them to accomplish the work of governing. Huntington, working quietly behind the scenes, persuaded the states to fulfil their promises for provisions and men for the army.

As an aside, Benedict Arnold became military governor of Philadelphia in 1778. It's not clear whether he and Huntington ever met, and it seems unlikely that they would have sought each other out. Arnold, who was ten years younger than Huntington, had moved to New Haven by the time Huntington arrived in Norwich, so they probably didn't know each other from home. Arnold's celebrity as a genuine military hero would certainly have reached Huntington's ears, but it seems unlikely that the reserved Huntington would have sought him out and even less likely that the arrogant Arnold would have approached the quiet lawyer. It seems curious, however, that Arnold apparently never approached Huntington or any of the Connecticut delegates to intervene when he was seeking promotions or during any of his difficulties with detractors.

Although he received no additional monetary compensation, the president was given a home, food and a household staff. Money became a problem, even for the plain-living Huntingtons, as they were expected to entertain foreign visitors and members of Congress while the salary from Congress didn't cover their own needs. Even with funds sent from Connecticut, there wasn't enough money to cover all the expenses. Their financial position was complicated by Samuel's absence from Norwich—if he was not at home, he couldn't tend to his law clients and earn the fees that would come in with the work.

Signing the Declaration of Independence. Engraving after a painting by John Trumbull. *Courtesy Library of Congress.*

The family's list of social activities was long and nearly constant. In December 1780, the entire French delegation was at Huntington's home for a formal banquet. The following May, he attended an entertainment for French and American officials given by the Chevalier de la Touche aboard the frigate *Hermione*.

Besides his work as leader of Congress, Huntington was still a delegate from Connecticut, so he would have been corresponding with Governor Trumbull and others back home to keep them apprised of congressional actions. By September 1780, Huntington was ready to return to Norwich, but he agreed to stay in Congress when he was elected to another term as its president.

Ratification of the Articles of Confederation had stalled over Maryland's concern about ownership of western land. Connecticut's original charter set the state's western border at the Pacific Ocean. New York and Virginia also relied on charters to claim land in what became known as the Western Reserve in present-day Ohio. Huntington's meetings with officials in each state eventually convinced them of the futility of continuing claims based on a grant from a king who no longer ruled over the state or the land in question. Ceding the land to the new nation was a better choice for the country, he suggested. With the question resolved, Maryland ratified the Articles of Confederation on March 1, 1781. Ratification became final with Maryland's vote, and Samuel Huntington became the first "President of the United States in Congress Assembled."

It seems safe to assume President Huntington felt a great sense of pride and, probably, relief when he wrote to the governors of the thirteen states:

> *By the Act of Congress herewith enclosed your Excellency will be informed that the Articles of Confederation & perpetual Union between the thirteen United States are formally & finally ratified by all the states. We are happy to congratulate our Constituents on this important Event, desired by our Friends but dreaded by our Enemies.*

As president of Congress, Huntington presided over its deliberations. The position would also have entailed attending many meetings and writing hundreds of letters on military matters—including getting states to provide men and supplies. In addition, the president handled mail service, economics and currency and whatever else came before Congress. Being president also meant wrangling sometimes uncooperative delegates to maintain a quorum to conduct business.

It was only a few months later that Huntington became ill and felt obligated to resign from Congress. At home in Norwich, he received a letter from fellow delegate John Witherspoon of New Jersey, who had become a friend. Witherspoon wrote,

> *With great satisfaction I observe by the public papers, the joyful and honorable reception you met with on your arrival, so expressive of that affection and approbation which to you will be the most grateful tribute of praise your country can bestow, and next to your consciousness of your having labored how to establish liberties of America, will be the greatest happiness you can enjoy.*

Connecticut elected Huntington to Congress in 1782, but he declined, citing uncertainties of his health and the demands of his position in the Superior Court. When he was elected again a year later, he accepted, and he arrived in Congress in July 1783, in time to rejoice two months later at the signing of the Treaty of Paris and the end of the war between the United States and Great Britain.

Although his term in Congress had ended, Huntington was not yet finished serving Connecticut. He was elected Connecticut's lieutenant governor in 1785. A year later, he was reelected, but when no candidate won a majority of the vote for governor, the election went to the General Assembly, which chose Samuel Huntington.

One of the state's most pressing problems was repairing the financial damage it had sustained during the Revolution. Through Huntington's work with the General Assembly, Connecticut established tax exemptions and other incentives for new industries such as textiles and established procedures for handling the claims of those injured during the war. This included awards of land in the Western Reserve. Connecticut withheld half a million acres of its relinquished claim to compensate citizens whose property had been burned by the British during the war. It was first called the Fire Suffers' Lands, which was later shortened to the Firelands. The sale of the remainder of that reserve was used to establish a permanent school fund for Connecticut.

While Huntington was governor, Connecticut established its first banks, established the country's first copyright law, barred the slave trade, began planning a statehouse in Hartford (now known as the Old State House) and took the first step toward separating churches and the government, which would permit residents to divert their tax money to dissenting churches.

Between 1785 and 1787, Dartmouth and Yale conferred upon Huntington honorary law degrees, in recognition of his service to state and country.

Samuel Huntington spoke to Connecticut's constitutional convention as it considered adopting the proposed United States Constitution in 1788. He welcomed hearing opinions that differed from his own, he said, and spoke of the need for representative government and two branches of legislature, specifically noting that one should be a check on the other. He advocated for a strong national government with enough power to deal with "matters of national concern." Connecticut voted by a wide margin to adopt the new Constitution.

Connecticut's freemen continued to elect Samuel Huntington as their governor until his death on January 5, 1796. Newspapers described the funeral procession to the church on the Green, where the Reverend Joseph Strong, Huntington's friend and pastor, conducted the service, which was attended by a large number of dignitaries, friends and neighbors. President and Governor Samuel Huntington was laid to rest next to Martha in a crypt in the Old Colonial Burying Ground, which was located just behind their home.

Chapter 7

WILLIAM WILLIAMS (1731–1811)

"I Have Signed the Declaration of Independence. I Shall Be Hung."

William Williams is perhaps the least known of Connecticut's signers of the Declaration of Independence. There are schools named for Oliver Wolcott and Samuel Huntington and a Connecticut town named for Roger Sherman. As for Williams, his home, now the William Williams House in Lebanon, appears to be the sole edifice bearing the signer's name.

After Philadelphia, Sherman served in both the national house and senate. Huntington and Wolcott were both governors of Connecticut. Williams returned to his positions in the Town of Lebanon, the Connecticut General Assembly and the Windham County courts. Although Williams had a long career in public service, the highest office he held was speaker of the lower house in the Connecticut legislature. It was a powerful position, to be sure, but the speaker is not generally well known.

It should be noted that Colonel William Williams of Lebanon, signer of the Declaration of Independence and judge of the Windham County courts, is not to be confused with General William Williams of Norwich, merchant and veteran of the War of 1812. He was a distant cousin, born in Stonington in 1788.

William Williams the signer was born in Lebanon, Connecticut, in 1731. The exact date is unclear because of discrepancies among records; different sources provide different dates in March and April. John Stark, author of the 1976 biography *Connecticut Signer: William Williams*, gives the date of March 18. Williams was the fourth son of the Reverend Solomon

Williams and Mary Porter Williams. Solomon Williams was pastor of the First Congregational Church in Lebanon. He himself was the son of the Reverend William Williams (1665–1741) of Hatfield, Massachusetts. Mary hailed from the nearby town of Hadley. A graduate of Yale, Solomon Williams was regarded as one of the leading religious figures in Connecticut and was a member of the Corporation of Yale College, the equivalent of a board of trustees.

William attended a local school and, intending to become a minister, followed in his father's footsteps to graduate from Harvard College in Massachusetts. William was granted a master's degree from Harvard in 1754. Apparently in deference to his father, William was awarded an ad eundem degree by Yale in 1753. According to Harvard's website, such degrees were granted to "persons who by courtesy were admitted without examination to the same degree (*ad eundum gradum*) that they had earned at some other institution." Two of William's brothers graduated from Yale.

With his schooling complete, William returned home to study with his father to prepare for his career in the ministry. He changed his mind, however, and opted to become a merchant. Around the same time, he also became interested in politics. When the incumbent town clerk died suddenly, William Williams was elected town clerk and town treasurer of Lebanon. He was only twenty-one when he was first elected to the office he would hold for the next forty-four years. The town clerk maintains all the town's records—births, marriages, deaths, land sales, deeds and minutes of the town meeting—which put Williams at the heart of the town's affairs.

Williams served on the staff of his cousin Colonel Ephraim Williams on an expedition to Crown Point, New York, in 1754–55 during the French and Indian War. At the Battle of Lake George on September 8, 1755, Colonel Williams was shot in the head in an ambush by the French and their Indian allies. In his will, Ephraim Williams provided funds to establish a school, which later became Williams College in Williamstown, Massachusetts. At least one biography suggests that William Williams's dislike of the British originated from his time in the militia, where the British officers apparently regarded the colonists as inferior beings.

William returned to Lebanon and opened his shop. In 1752, at the age of twenty-one, he was elected selectman and became the town's chief executive officer. He would be reelected twenty-seven times. It wasn't unusual for a townsman to fill several positions, and in fact, William added several others. He was elected to the General Assembly of Connecticut in 1757, and voters returned him there, for all but three years, until 1776. Members of the house were suitably impressed by Williams's abilities, and in 1766, he was elected clerk of the house. Back in Lebanon, Williams was chosen as major of the town militia group. Two years later, his adamant devotion to traditional Congregational beliefs brought him appointment as deacon of the church.

William Williams, signer of the Declaration of Independence. *Courtesy the New York Public Library Digital Collection.*

Williams held himself to a high standard in his personal, business and political dealings, and he expected the same from other people. He was described as a man of medium height with pleasing, well-proportioned features and a powerful voice. Stark notes, however, that Williams's high standards for others, his deep piety and his natural reserve and taciturnity gave him the reputation—particularly among those whose standards were lower—"of being a self-righteous prig." Stark goes on to note that this reputation may have been deserved, as Williams "had absolute faith in the justice and virtue of his own position and was intolerant of those whose political opinions and motives seemed less pure than his own."

For all that Williams was involved in state and national affairs, it appears his was a remarkably parochial outlook. He wasn't widely traveled and rarely left Connecticut. He had few correspondents beyond Connecticut's borders and didn't trust people who weren't New Englanders. Despite all that, Williams apparently had a romantic side. On February 14, 1771, he married Mary Trumbull, second daughter of Governor Jonathan Trumbull. He was forty; she was twenty-five. The marriage would have helped his political ambitions, but their letters suggest there was genuine caring between them. He worried over the health of his "dearest Polly" and cautioned her not to overexert herself, longed to be home, urged her to write more often; she wrote of how much she liked hearing from him (Mary apparently found writing letters difficult).

According to Stark, this was not William's first romantic attachment. His papers include letters, apparently unsent, expressing romantic feeling to at least two women, one of whom was Faith Trumbull, Mary's older sister, who married Jedidiah Huntington of Norwich.

William Williams became a leader of the opposition to Parliament's attempts to control the colonies. He was involved with the Sons of Liberty in their opposition to the Stamp Act and wrote Lebanon's 1768 letter responding to John Dickinson's "Letters from a Farmer," endorsing Dickinson's objections to Parliament using taxes to raise revenue. The next year, the town adopted a resolution supporting the non-importation of British goods, and in 1770, Williams was adamant about the necessity of strict adherence to non-importation to save America from "compleat slavery." By the time he was thirty, William Williams was recognized as one of the half-dozen leading figures in the Town of Lebanon.

As always, local political maneuvering went on despite national events. The Connecticut religious community had been split in the 1730s, the period known as the Great Awakening. Ministers such as Jonathan Edwards of Northampton, Massachusetts, preached a "New Light" of faith that seemed quite emotional compared to the formality of the Old Light/traditional worship. The differences extended into politics, and the conservative Old Lighters mounted a continuing campaign to dominate the colony's political offices.

Richard Bushman, author of *From Puritan to Yankee*, suggests the New Lights viewed the British policy as a "conspiracy aimed at the destruction of Liberty." Coincidentally, many of the New Lighters hailed from eastern Connecticut. Over the next decade, the number of New Light adherents steadily increased until they held a majority in the lower house of the legislature.

Following the Boston Massacre on March 5, 1770, Williams and Joshua West were dispatched to New Haven on September 13 as representatives to a general convention on the non-importation agreements. The repeal of the Townshend Acts effectively mooted the non-importation agreements, prompting farmers in the eastern part of Connecticut to condemn the abandonment of principle for profit.

Although Williams was a shareholder in the Susquehanna Company, he seemed indifferent as the issue resolved itself with support from the New Lights who headed the government, but it may be that national events overshadowed local and regional issues.

When the British closed the Port of Boston following the Boston Tea Party, Williams led Lebanon in expressing its support for Boston. On June 1, the day the Port of Boston was closed, Lebanon observed a day of mourning. That evening, Williams's elderly father, the Reverend Solomon Williams, introduced at the town meeting a proclamation pledging the town's support for Boston and the cause of American liberty. The town meeting was unanimous in its vote of support.

The younger Williams turned his considerable talent to essays and letters to the newspapers urging support for the cause of liberty. He urged the town and militia officers to increase their store of guns, powder and bullets and ensure that all militia officers had the proper equipment.

Three hundred of Lebanon's citizens attended a town meeting on July 18 and declared that Boston's cause was the cause of all America. They pledged to support the Congress if it ended trade with Britain and then appointed a six-member Committee of Correspondence, whose members included William Williams and his brother-in-law Jonathan Trumbull Jr. Lebanon was diligent in providing aid to Boston—including money and a flock of 376 sheep. Later, the townspeople sent £30 worth of cattle, and even more aid was sent into the next year.

Williams continued to press his ideas about preparedness as he was elected speaker of the house in October 1774. He promptly began advocating for increasing military training and defense, including doubling the stockpile of ammunition and even proper carriages for cannon to defend the shoreline town of New London. By the beginning of 1775, Williams, speaking for the Connecticut Committee of Correspondence, could report, with some satisfaction, that "the people of this colony are more and more united" as they moved toward separation from England.

In his 1829 *Character Sketch from Lives of the Signers of the Declaration of Independence*, the Reverend Charles A. Goodrich notes that Williams's time in the military left him with lessons he did not forget. "He was at that time disgusted with the British commanders, on account of the haughtiness of their conduct, and the little attachment which they manifested for his native country," Goodrich wrote, adding Williams was convinced that "America would see no days of prosperity and peace, so long as British officers should manage her affairs."

Recognizing the demands that would be made on his time, Williams closed his shop in Lebanon and devoted himself to preparing for war. This, of course, meant he would have no income except whatever he might be paid for his government positions. Goodrich notes that this was not the only sacrifice Williams made for his country. During the early part of the war, prospective soldiers declined to enlist as the paper money printed by the colony had so little value that they would be fighting for no pay at all. When Williams exchanged more than $2,000 in hard money for the all-but-worthless paper, he had little hope of recouping his investment, and he accepted that. Williams continued his writings warning of looming war and preaching preparedness.

By March 1775, the legislature was making it known that there would be no place in Connecticut for British loyalists or Tories, as they were called. The Connecticut General Assembly launched an investigation of militia officers accused of being British sympathizers and sent out a committee "to examine affairs in the Tory towns of Ridgefield and Newtown," as Stark put it.

After British troops and American militiamen clashed at Lexington and Concord on April 19, 1775, forty-nine Connecticut towns sent men to Boston. On behalf of Connecticut's Committee of Correspondence, Williams wrote to John Hancock in Massachusetts to reiterate Connecticut's support for Boston.

A special session of the assembly responded to Williams's urgings by appointing Joseph Trumbull commissary general, to head efforts to acquire necessities for an army, print $50,000 worth of paper money and appoint overseers of powder and cannon. The assembly also banned the export of provisions from the state.

The regular session of the assembly, which convened on May 11, sent four regiments of Connecticut troops to Massachusetts and adopted official articles of war. Members also ordered the printing of another $50,000 of paper money and removed three Tory militia officers. Additionally, Sparks notes, they passed a measure that encouraged domestic manufacture of military supplies and created a Council of Safety to assist the governor.

Williams found himself with an additional workload as a member both of the nine-member Council of Safety and of a seven-member committee charged with obtaining guns and encouraging their manufacture. Then, when the judge of Windham's Probate Court became ill, the assembly appointed Williams to fill the position. Around the same time, Williams was made colonel of the Twelfth Regiment when its commander was appointed commander of all the Connecticut forces in Massachusetts.

The Council of Safety was given the task of directing military and naval operations of Connecticut troops as well as the authority to send Connecticut troops to other colonies. Like the national congress, the committee could become embroiled in soothing the hurt feelings that ensued when a younger officer was promoted over a veteran. In July, Williams and Samuel Huntington had the job of persuading General Joseph Spencer to stay in the army after he threatened to resign because Congress promoted Israel Putnam to major general (in the Continental army) while Spencer was a brigadier, even though he had held the higher rank in the militia.

Stark counted more than 1,000 meetings of the Council of Safety. Williams was present at 622 of those meetings, which Stark characterized as more meetings than anyone else except the governor.

One measure of the assembly's trust in Williams was manifested when he was sent with Eliphalet Dyer to Philadelphia to seek reimbursement from Congress for Connecticut's war expenditures. They returned a month later with $166,666 for the Connecticut treasury.

When the assembly met in October 1775, Silas Deane and Eliphalet Dyer were recalled from the Continental Congress at Philadelphia. Members named Oliver Wolcott and Samuel Huntington to replace them and Titus Hosmer and William Williams as alternates. According to Stark, the relationship between Williams and Dyer was "chilly," while Williams and Deane "detested each other." Deane and Sherman disliked each other, and Dyer had enemies of his own. Although there were others with negative feelings about him, Deane blamed Williams—whom he described as a "little malevolent prig in buckram"—for the ouster.

Citing letters from the collected papers of both Adams and Deane, Stark suggests that Williams distrusted Deane and had apparently warned Samuel Adams that Deane was "not genuine." In Williams's eyes, Deane's patriotism was not sincere devotion to the cause; rather, it was driven by his self-interest as a merchant. This appears to have been the result of Williams's deep religious conviction and New Light beliefs, which brought him to his dogged political devotion to the American cause. Williams wrote that if the American cause required "the last farthing I have, She is double welcome, 'tis much better expended than to support the Tyrant Lords who will succeed the Loss of Liberty."

As speaker of the house, Williams may have had a major role in one of the great ironies in the history of Connecticut. In December 1775, the assembly passed a law stating that people who gave aid and comfort to the enemy could be imprisoned and forfeit their estates. Anyone who spoke against congress or the assembly lost all political privileges. This created a situation in which a British colony (as Connecticut still was) criminalized residents who were loyal to Britain.

When delegates left for Philadelphia in April, all indications were that Connecticut strongly favored independence, but the General Assembly had not yet taken a formal vote, and thus the delegates had no instructions on the question. It was not until June 14 that the General Assembly directed "that the Delegates of his Colony in General Congress be and they are hereby instructed to propose to that respectable body, to declare the

United American Colonies Free and Independent States, absolved from all allegiance to the King of Great Britain."

In fact, Williams was not in Philadelphia for the July 4, 1776 vote on the Declaration of Independence. Word of independence didn't come to Connecticut until July 11, prompting the Council of Safety to decide that Connecticut needed full representation in the Congress. Oliver Wolcott was sick, so the Council moved alternate delegate Williams to full delegate status. Williams left on July 22 for a six-day journey in what apparently was hot, sultry weather, made worse by an attack of what he called "the quick Step" (an army term for diarrhea) when he arrived. Williams signed the formal document declaring independence on August 2.

Williams was a conscientious, if reluctant, delegate to the Congress in Philadelphia. Stark describes him as a delegate of secondary importance who neither held a key position nor had a role in formulating policy. He was assigned to committees for revision of the journals of Congress and oversight of their printing, purchasing blankets and clothing for soldiers and preparing a plan for a military academy.

Williams was in Philadelphia in July and August 1776 when Congress began to draft the Articles of Confederation. It was, he said, "slow progress.... Every Inch of Ground is disputed." Others must have shared his sentiment, as Congress soon dropped discussion of the articles because antagonism was too deep. It may have been just as well, as the British troops were drawing close. Congress evacuated Philadelphia on September 18, and a week later, British General William Howe entered the city.

Williams returned to Lebanon to resume his state and local duties, in all likelihood closely following the progress of the war. Toward the close of 1776, it was not going well for the Americans, and fears were growing about the outcome. The Council of Safety was called to meet in Lebanon, and two members, William Hillhouse of Montville and Benjamin Huntington of Norwich, stayed with Williams. Goodrich describes a scene in which their conversation turned to the "gloomy state of the country, and the probability that, after all, success would crown the British arms."

> *"Well," said Mr. Williams, with great calmness, "if they succeed, it is pretty evident what will be my fate. I have done much to prosecute the contest, and one thing I have done, which the British will never pardon—I have signed the Declaration of Independence. I shall be hung."*
>
> *Mr. Hillhouse expressed his hope, that America would yet be successful, and his confidence that this would be her happy fortune.*

IN CONGRESS, JULY 4, 1776.

The unanimous Declaration of the thirteen united States of America,

This is the document that proclaimed America's independence from Britain. *Courtesy Library of Congress*

> *Mr. Huntington observed, that in case of ill success, he should be exempt from the gallows, as his signature was not attached to the Declaration of Independence, nor had he written anything against the British government.*
>
> *To this Mr. Williams replied, his eye kindling as he spoke, "Then, sir, you deserve to be hanged, for not having done your duty."*

Congress again took up the Articles of Confederation in April 1777 and worked through disagreements about apportionment of taxes—to be assessed by the population of a state or by the value of its land? —and sent a completed document to the states in November. Williams declared himself satisfied and voted in favor of adopting the articles, which were then sent to the states. Governor Trumbull ordered three hundred copies printed for distribution to the towns. Lebanon was among forty-five Connecticut towns that explicitly approved the Articles of Confederation. The lower house of the General Assembly approved the articles in January and the upper house in February.

Williams was in New Haven for a session of the General Assembly in 1781 when he learned that French troops were coming to Lebanon for the winter and he would be quartering a Colonel Dillon. Given his dislike of the French and anything outside of Connecticut, Williams was upset but apparently didn't refuse. He and Mary were appalled by the extravagance, vanity and arrogance of the French officers and more so by behavior of the French troops, who fought, cut down trees, stole animals and more. They did not regret the departure of the French soldiers.

On September 6, 1781, a few weeks before the Battle of Yorktown, Connecticut's most infamous resident returned. Benedict Arnold, now a general in the British army, was commanding troops that would attack Fort Griswold in Groton and, across the Thames River, burn New London. Legend has it that Williams rode twenty-six miles to New London in three hours, apparently intending to join the fight. Stark notes that letters Williams wrote in the evening on September 6 and the morning on September 7 contain no reference to such an event. Williams received information about the fighting from an express rider and forwarded the news to Governor Trumbull without any suggestion that he was an eyewitness.

After the war ended, Williams continued his work in Connecticut government and the courts. In 1788, he served as a delegate to the ratifying convention at Hartford to consider Connecticut's adoption of the Constitution of the United States. He voted for it, although he objected to the clause forbidding religious tests. His later years were spent as a county judge. His career in the assembly ended in 1803, and he relinquished his court positions in 1805. By 1810, Williams admitted, he was having difficulty walking without a cane. His son Solomon died in 1810, and apparently, Williams never recovered from the loss. He himself died on August 2, 1811, in Lebanon and is buried in the Trumbull Cemetery in eastern Lebanon.

Chapter 8
THE TRUMBULLS

Joseph Trumbull (1737–1778)

Commissary General of Stores and Provisions

He thought he might become General George Washington's secretary. But the general had another idea after he noticed how well Connecticut's supply line worked while the state's troops were outside Boston in 1775 and sought out Connecticut's commissary general to head the supply department for the entire Continental army.

Joseph Trumbull was appointed the first commissary general of stores and provisions for the Continental army, with the rank of colonel, and served in that position from July 19, 1775, to August 2, 1777. A few years before, Trumbull bought a house on East Town Street in Norwich, a few doors down from his sister and brother-in-law, Faith and Jedidiah Huntington, and his cousin Samuel Huntington. Joseph Trumbull's friend Eliphalet Dyer, a member of Congress, proposed Joseph to the general as a secretary. Dyer wrote to Trumbull to describe what he had done without his friend's knowledge, confident he would like the general. The general, in turn, recommended Trumbull to Congress, and Congress honored his wishes.

The commissary position was probably a much better fit than being Washington's secretary for Trumbull, who had been a partner with his father in the family mercantile and trading business, giving him experience in moving food and goods from one place to another.

Colonel Joseph Trumbull, chief provisioner of the Continental army. *Courtesy the New York Public Library Digital Collection.*

Joseph Trumbull was the eldest child of Jonathan Trumbull Sr. and Faith (Robinson) Trumbull, born on March 11, 1737. Like his father, he graduated from Harvard College, became a prosperous merchant and even practiced law for a short time. In 1763, Trumbull joined the militia as a captain in the Twelfth Connecticut Regiment. He also served six years in Connecticut's General Assembly, four years of that time while his father was governor. Although he was appointed an alternate delegate to the First Continental Congress, he didn't attend any sessions.

In the *Journal of the American Revolution*, David Price wrote,

> *The enormity of the assignment facing Trumbull when he assumed his duties was staggering. He had to frantically organize butchers, bakers, storekeepers, and purchasing agents while recruiting coopers to assemble barrels for preserved pork and beef and the increasingly scarce salt needed to cure that meat, which in some cases was found to be horse flesh.*

Trumbull went to work creating a supply system, and after a year, General Washington was able to write to John Hancock that "few armies, if any, have been better and more plentifully supplied than the troops under Mr. Trumbull's care."

Yet after this initial success, supplying adequate provisions became increasingly difficult, according to Price. The lack of money was always a problem; most farmers would accept only hard currency. This put Trumbull at a disadvantage against the British and even state commissaries who were competing for the same provisions. Transportation difficulties, such as lack of adequate wagons to deliver the supplies or roads so bad the wagons couldn't traverse them, added to the difficulties.

The biggest problem remained money, and finally, Trumbull was reduced to borrowing from Connecticut. He devised a plan to use water transport to bring flour from Virginia and meat by wagon from New England to feed the army. And always, Trumbull was haunted by the prospect of soldiers starving if he couldn't meet the demand for provisions.

In March 1777, Trumbull married Amelia Dyer of Windham, daughter of his friend Eliphalet Dyer. Three months later, in June 1777, Trumbull resigned as commissary general, as Congress had divided his position in a way that would make it impossible for him to properly do his job. In November, he was appointed to the Board of War, and he held that position until April 1778, when he resigned because of illness. On July 23, 1778, Joseph Trumbull died at home in Lebanon. He is buried in the East Cemetery in Lebanon.

Jonathan Trumbull (1710–1785)

Governor of Connecticut Colony, Then Governor of Connecticut State

Jonathan Trumbull of Connecticut was one of only two men to serve as both governor of a British colony and governor of an American state. The other was Nicholas Cooke of Rhode Island. Of the two, only Trumbull supported the patriot cause at the start of the war. His support of the war as well as family relationships frequently brought him to Norwich. His daughter Faith married Jedidiah Huntington, who became active in the Sons of Liberty and the militia. Jedidiah's father was major general of Connecticut's militia, and Trumbull's oldest son, Joseph, lived in Norwich a few houses away from Faith and Jedidiah.

The future governor was born on October 12, 1710, in Lebanon, Connecticut. His parents were Joseph Trumble and Hannah Higley. It was the governor who changed the spelling of his name from Trumble to Trumbull around 1765. Joseph Trumble moved to Lebanon about five years before Jonathan's birth and established an importing and trading business. Jonathan helped in the business until he was thirteen, when he went to Harvard to study for the ministry. By 1730, he had earned a master's degree and been licensed by the Congregational church. Although he may have preached a few times and was considered as a candidate, he never became an ordained minister.

Jonathan Trumbull became a merchant with his father in 1731, participating more fully in the business after the death of his brother at sea in 1732. Within a year of Jonathan's leaving Harvard, he and his elder brother Joseph opened a trading partnership. They brought livestock and other items from Lebanon to Boston and other cities, traded them for merchandise imported from Europe and returned to Lebanon to sell their cargo. Joseph disappeared while on a trading voyage in 1732, leaving Jonathan the sole proprietor.

In 1733, Lebanon sent Jonathan to the General Assembly, and he became a colonel in the colonial militia. Around the same time, he began studying law. Two years later, on December 9, 1735, Jonathan married seventeen-year-old Faith Robinson, daughter of the Reverend John Robinson and Hannah Wiswell Robinson, who lived in Duxbury, Massachusetts. Their six children were Joseph Trumbull (1737–1778), Jonathan Trumbull Jr. (1740–1809), Faith (1743–1775), Mary (1745–1831), David (1751–1822) and John (1756–1843).

While Joseph Trumbull became commissary general of Connecticut during the Revolutionary War, his brother Jonathan Jr. served in the army and later became governor himself; his sister Faith married Jedidah Huntington of Norwich, who commanded Connecticut troops during the war; Mary married William Williams, the Lebanon merchant who represented Connecticut in Congress and was a signer of the Declaration of Independence; David was commissary of Connecticut and father of Joseph Trumbull, the state's thirty-fifth governor; and John served in the army but became better known as the Painter of the American Revolution.

Over twenty years, Jonathan Trumbull Sr. served multiple terms in the General Assembly and was speaker of the house in 1739, 1752 and 1754. He also served as justice of the peace and judge of the county, superior and probate courts of Windham County before his appointment as chief justice of Connecticut's Superior Court from 1766 to 1769 while serving as the colony's lieutenant governor. Trumbull was appointed governor to complete the term of William Pitkin, who died on October 1, 1769. In the next election, Trumbull received more votes than the other candidates, but the election went to the legislature as no candidate had more than 50 percent of the vote. The legislature appointed Jonathan Trumbull, who was reelected as colonial governor until 1776 and as governor of Connecticut until 1784.

Trumbull had a somewhat spotty record as a businessman. During the French and Indian War, he did well as a supplier to the troops. After the war, his profits dwindled, apparently because he was overly generous in extending credit to his customers, as one historian put it. It is estimated that in 1763, he had $10,000 in outstanding bills that remained unpaid while his creditors sought payment from him. Why he allowed that to happen is unclear, but there is some suggestion that Trumbull appreciated the goodwill of his customers—and their votes in the next election—more than he valued a healthy balance sheet. It should be noted, however, that regardless of his merit as a businessman, the consensus is that Trumbull was precisely the right man for the governorship during the difficult years of the Revolution.

Trumbull was credited with the ability to work with people on all sides of an issue. A major issue in Connecticut in the mid-1700s was which religious group would run the state. The Great Awakening of the 1830s and '40s had taken hold and split the population into "New Lights" and "Old Lights." The New Light preachers advocated for a new sense of piety—a New Light—and held that everyone is a sinner whose salvation depends on a merciful God. Their sermons were emotional and often leaned toward what we might today call fire and brimstone. The Old Lights were the establishment ministers, particularly in areas dominated by the Congregational church, who questioned the excesses of the revivalists and their mass meetings and objected to women and African Americans speaking to religious gatherings.

The division spilled over into government as the new churches advocated for an end to state support of churches—both Congregationalism in Connecticut and Massachusetts and the Anglican church that was favored in the South. Jonathan Trumbull managed to navigate the division without alienating either side. He proposed a bill in 1743 that banned ministers from entering parishes without invitation, a nod to the Old Lights. In eastern Connecticut, the area of his strongest support, Trumbull was, however, generally regarded as attuned to the New Lights. In the 1760s, he was a shareholder in the Susquehanna Company and supported its efforts to establish a settlement in Pennsylvania and was also a supporter of the Sons of Liberty as they formed to resist what they perceived as the British tyranny evidenced by increasingly painful taxation of the colonists.

Trumbull's role changed dramatically after the Declaration of Independence. The General Assembly recognized that Connecticut would need a strong executive during the war and granted Trumbull the authority that would be necessary. In 1774, Governor Trumbull refused a request from British General Thomas Gage to send Connecticut militiamen to help the British after the fighting at Lexington and Concord. He is quoted as replying that the British troops would "disgrace even barbarians." Gage himself, he said, made a "most unprovoked attack" on the Americans, who were still His Majesty's subjects. And thus Trumbull became the only colonial governor to side with the patriots. The Trumbull store in Lebanon became a war office and served as the meeting place for the Council of Safety, most of whose members were from eastern Connecticut.

The governor became a close friend and an advisor to George Washington, who relied on Connecticut for what's estimated to have been 60 percent of the supplies needed for his army, earning for Connecticut the sobriquet "the Provision State." According to the Connecticut Historical Society, George Washington, the Marquis de Lafayette, Rochambeau, Benjamin Franklin, Samuel and John Adams, Thomas Jefferson and Generals Putnam and Knox are among those believed to have visited Trumbull in Lebanon. Legend has it that during meetings, Washington would turn to Trumbull and ask what "Brother Jonathan" had to say on the matter.

Connecticut's western land claims were a recurring question during the Trumbull administrations. In the fall of 1776, the assembly established the county of Westmoreland in present-day Pennsylvania, and seven years later, Trumbull cited the 1662 charter in asserting Connecticut's right to all the land granted in the charter. Connecticut eventually relinquished that claim, although a portion of the western land (now Ohio) was retained to reimburse residents whose property was destroyed by the British during the war. After those claims were settled, the remainder of the land was sold. Proceeds from the sale were placed in a Common School Fund to help establish public education throughout the state.

During the war, Trumbull acted as the Northen Department paymaster for the Continental army but resigned following his mother's death. He asked that his back pay be distributed to the soldiers of that department.

Trumbull's popularity began to wane as the war continued. He wanted to ban price controls; rumors were spread that he was personally profiting from trade with British-held areas; he wasn't so sure about the idea of equality for all. In 1784, Trumbull declined to seek another term as governor, which was probably a wise decision since, according to records, he had not received the 50 percent of votes necessary for election in three of the previous four elections. Governor Trumbull suffered a stroke at his Lebanon home and died on August 17, 1785. He is buried in a tomb at Trumbull Cemetery in Lebanon. His home and the war office are now museums.

The governor was not without his share of honors. He was admitted as an honorary member of the Society of the Cincinnati and awarded honorary degrees from Yale and the University of Edinburgh.

Unlike some of his contemporaries, Jonathan Trumbull is remembered at home and across the state. Lebanon's public library bears his name, as does the Town of Trumbull in Connecticut and Trumbull County in Ohio, as well as streets in New Haven and Hartford. Fort Trumbull in

New London is named for the governor, and so is Trumbull College at Yale University and Trumbull House on the University of Connecticut campus in Storrs. Perhaps best known of all the Trumbull namesakes is the University of Connecticut's mascot: a husky named Jonathan, for Connecticut's best-known governor.

CHAPTER 9

OTHER NORWICH HEROES

Norwich's participation in the Revolutionary War was not confined to prominent citizens who became generals and members of Congress. Tradesmen, laborers and free African Americans also volunteered to serve.

There also were some citizens who wanted to avoid service or perhaps were unable to be away from home. A lesser-known practice during the Revolutionary War was enlisting enslaved men in the army as a way to meet a town's recruitment quota. Others were sent as a replacement for the master. Some of the enslaved were given the promise of freedom on their return; others weren't so lucky.

One of the exciting things about studying history is the new discoveries that are constantly emerging. Sometimes an overlooked piece of paper in a file reveals new information about a well-known subject. Other times, researchers look at areas that were not previously studied. In recent years, more attention is being devoted to the enslaved men and Native Americans who served in the Continental army. Because they weren't prominent, little information is available about them. The following stories are about some of the men for whom information is available.

DR PHILIP TURNER (1740–1815)

"A Natural Insight into Wounds"

Dr. Philip Turner, army surgeon. *Collection of the author.*

Before he ever went off to war, Dr. Philip Turner found himself in a war at home. He found himself fighting the government to save the lives of the people under his care. Dr. Turner was regarded as an "exceptionally fine surgeon," according to historian Nafie. That reputation didn't necessarily help him when it came to discussions about smallpox vaccination, which was a major medical issue during the War for Independence.

Philip Turner was born in Norwich in 1738, the son of Philip Turner, who came to Norwich from Scituate, Massachusetts, and Anna Huntington, daughter of Daniel Huntington and granddaughter of Deacon Simon Huntington. Anna was previously married to Thomas Adgate, grandson of another Norwich founder, with whom she had several children.

After Philip's parents died when he was young, Dr. Elisha Tracy became his foster father and mentor. Caulkins's *History* notes that at age twenty, Turner enlisted in the army as an assistant surgeon and served on the "northern frontier," meaning Fort Ticonderoga and upstate New York, with John Durkee's troops during the French and Indian War. He continued to serve until the end of the war. After leaving the army in 1763, Turner married Dr. Tracy's daughter Lucy, with whom he had seven children, including his daughter Nancy, who married Marvin Wait. Their son John Turner Wait (1811–1899) served in the United States Congress.

While Dr. Turner was still practicing medicine in Norwich, he became ensnared in one of the biggest controversies of the time: smallpox inoculation. Smallpox was among the deadliest and most widespread diseases of the time. It is a highly contagious viral illness that causes fever, nausea, vomiting and pustules (or pox) on the body. It was often fatal; at the least, it could be debilitating. In the close quarters of the army, it could be devastating, both for individuals and for troop strength—as smallpox swept through the ranks, fewer soldiers would be able for duty.

As early as 1721, Dr. Cotton Mather, the noted Boston clergyman who also engaged in medicine, began advocating for inoculation in Boston as a means of stopping the spread of the disease. The process was fairly simple: pus was removed from an active pustule on an infected person and then inserted into a small cut or scratch on the skin of a healthy person to induce a mild case of the disease that would result in immunity.

In 1760, Norwich's Dr. Elisha Lord proposed inoculating for smallpox, and the question was put to a vote at the town meeting, which voted no. In 1773, Dr. Turner and Dr. Jonathan Loomis opened a hospital for inoculation on an island off Stonington on the Connecticut coast. Caulkins described such increasing hostility from mainland residents that Drs. Turner and Loomis closed the facility. Dr. Loomis was imprisoned in 1774, charged with spreading smallpox by infecting two people via inoculation. When he escaped after a few days, the authorities responded as if he were a hardened criminal. Even Turner's mentor Dr. Tracy, well regarded as honorable and skillful, was brought before a grand jury on charges he communicated smallpox by inoculation.

In 1775, Dr. Turner headed to Massachusetts after the fighting at Lexington and Concord and joined the army. He served as a military surgeon for Jedidah Huntington's Eighth Connecticut Regiment at the Battle of Bunker Hill. Turner remained with the army until his enlistment expired in December. The following spring, he reenlisted and was present at White Plains, Harlem, Danbury and other battles. In 1777, Dr. Turner was appointed surgeon general of the Continental army's Eastern Department.

When the war ended, Dr. Turner returned to Norwich and resumed his medical practice. He soon developed a reputation as a leading surgeon in the area, if not the entire state. This reputation aligns with what General Jedidiah Huntington wrote few years earlier: "Dr. Turner is blessed with a natural insight into wounds and a dexterity in handling them peculiar to himself." Dr. Turner moved his practice to New York City in 1800, where he was named staff surgeon for the United States Army and oversaw government hospitals.

Dr. Turner died in New York in 1815 and was buried in the cemetery at Trinity Church. There is some suggestion he was later reburied with his wife in Yantic Cemetery in Norwich.

Philip Turner's eldest son, John (1764–1837), was for many years a successful and well-known physician in Norwich, according to a 1928 article by Charles Graves, MD, in *Annals of Medical History*. A second son, William Pitt Turner, became a surgeon in New York City. Turner's daughter Lucy

Ann married Dr. Gurdon Lathrop of Norwich, who became a druggist as well as a physician. His daughter Elizabeth married Daniel Lathrop, son of Dr. Joshua Lathrop, who with his brother Daniel operated the apothecary shop on Upper Washington Street in Norwich.

Diah Manning (1760–1815)

The General's Bodyguard

Fifteen-year-old Diah Manning was among the Norwich men who enlisted in Colonel Jedidiah Huntington's Eighth Regiment when the fighting began. He was a drummer, assigned to the First Company commanded by Captain Thomas Kingsbury. His seventeen-year-old brother Roger, who was also a drummer, enlisted with him. Their father apparently served in the same regiment, according to the entry for the Manning family in *North American Family History*. Samuel Manning enlisted on July 22 and served until November 27, 1775. Diah enlisted on July 10 and served until December 16 with Huntington's militia.

The Mannings lived on Town Street in a house that abuts the road to the colonial cemetery. Samuel Manning's family originated in Massachusetts; he himself was born in Windham. Diah's mother, Anna Winship, was a descendant of an early Massachusetts family.

When George Washington assumed command, he reorganized the army, and Huntington's regiment became the First Connecticut Regiment of the Continental army. The next year, Washington ordered regimental commanding officers to select four men from each unit to serve in a special unit who would act as his bodyguards. Both Manning brothers were chosen. The general's order was specific on qualifications for selection: "good men who were sober, honest and well-behaved; five foot eight inches to five foot ten inches in height; handsomely and well-made," with particular attention to men who were clean and "spruce."

Although their official designation was the General's Guard, the group was popularly called the Life Guards. Their mission was to protect Washington as well as the army's cash and official papers. The Life Guards went to New York City with Washington, and before the end of 1776, a plot to assassinate the general was uncovered. Life Guard member Thomas Hickey persuaded several other members to join him in the plot, which was discovered when Hickey was arrested for counterfeiting. He apparently bragged to a cellmate, who reported the conversation to authorities. Hickey was court-martialed and executed by hanging on June 28, 1776.

The Life Guards fought in the Battle of White Plains and the Battle of Trenton in December 1776. When the army went into winter quarters, Washington reorganized the Life Guards into a new elite unit, according to an article on the website George Washington's Mount Vernon. Their new uniforms were blue and buff with leather helmets bound in blue fabric with a white plume on the left side. At the time, the regiment number appeared on uniform buttons. Buttons on Life Guard uniforms carried for the first time the designation "USA."

The Life Guards were with Washington at Valley Forge, and in the spring of 1778, Baron von Steuben chose the Life Guards as a demonstration unit for the drill he was teaching the army. They, in turn, were expected to work with the soldiers to help train them. This was considered "a testament to the unit's professionalism and military standards," the Mount Vernon website said.

As one of General Washington's Life Guards, Diah Manning was present for the events of September 1780, when Benedict Arnold's treason was discovered after the capture of John André. The British officer was taken to the Continental army headquarters at Tappan, New York. General Washington convened a court of inquiry whose members included General Jedidiah Huntington of Norwich. André was found guilty of being a spy and held in Tappan until October 2, the date set for his execution by hanging. It was Diah Manning, who became drum major of the Life Guards in 1778, who served the prisoner his breakfast on the last day, bringing the food directly from the general's table. Later, Manning joined the drummers who played the final march as André walked to the gallows.

Manning apparently remained in the army until at least 1783, when he was listed on a payroll showing his monthly pay as nine dollars (presumably Continentals). On April 27, 1784, Manning married Anna Gifford (1762–1851) of Norwich. They had six children: Samuel Manning (1785–1828), Johannah Manning Lillie (1788–1877), William Lord Manning (1791–1856), Asa Manning (1795–1879), Lemira Manning Spencer (1798–1875) and Joseph Terry Manning (1801–1852).

For the rest of his life, Manning was well known in Norwich for his close association with Washington. He was the sexton of the First Congregational Church and became the bellringer of Norwichtown.

In 1800, an American ship took a prize vessel carrying what were described as fugitives from the conflict between Saint-Domingue (now Haiti) and Santo Domingo (now the Dominican Republic), and the prisoners were taken to Norwich. Among them was a young man named Jean-Pierre Boyer, who lodged with the Manning family for about a year. Both Caulkins and Mary Perkins state that the family was very kind to the young man. Boyer later became president of Haiti, serving from 1818 to 1843. According to Caulkins, nearly twenty years after his stay in Norwich, Boyer remembered the Manning family's kindness to him and sent a "handsome gratuity" to the family. He sent $400 to Anna Manning and the widow of Consider Sterry.

Diah Manning died on August 25, 1815, at age fifty-five and is buried at the Old Colonial Burying Ground at the end of the lane next to his home. Roger Manning left the army in 1780 and returned home to become a teacher of drumming. According to *North American Family Histories, 1500–2000*, he went to sea on a privateer and was never heard from again once he passed New London, but no local (Norwich) mention of his fate has surfaced.

Samuel Ashbow Jr. (1746–1775)

The first Native American to die in the American Revolution was Samuel Ashbow Jr. of the Mohegan tribe. Samuel was born around 1746, one of four sons of the Reverend Samuel Ashbow and Hannah Mamanash. They lived in Norwich's North Parish, now Montville.

With his brother John, Samuel enlisted on May 10, 1775, in the Third Company under the command of Colonel John Durkee in Israel Putnam's Third Connecticut Regiment. Ashbow was killed during a British attack on the American redoubt in the Battle of Bunker Hill. According to the 2004 National Park Service study *Patriots of Color*, they were stationed at the rail fence. Like the four hundred other Americans who died that day, Ashbow is probably buried in a mass grave on or near the grounds of the Bunker Hill monument.

At the time of his death, Ashbow was married to a woman named Jerusha, according to the online Native Northeast Portal, an online collaboration to provide access to historical material about Native Americans. They had a son, Joshua, who was born in 1773.

Samuel Ashbow is depicted on a mural on the side of the Market Street parking garage in Norwich. The mural was a project of Public Art for Racial Justice Education, a Southeastern Connecticut coalition dedicated to raising awareness of racial justice issues through art.

Cato Mead (Circa 1761–1846)

Cato Mead's story comes to Norwich by way of Montrose, Iowa, and Minneapolis, Minnesota. In 1969, the Montrose Daughters of the American Revolution placed a monument to honor Cato Mead, a Revolutionary War soldier who died in their town. In 2006, Barbara MacLeish of Minneapolis discovered Mead as she was researching census records, which show him to have been a "free man of color."

Coincidentally, around the same time, U.S. Senator Christopher Dodd, a former Norwich resident, was a cosponsor of a bill to establish the National Liberty Memorial to honor the slaves and free African Americans who served during the Revolution.

Like Samuel Ashbow, Mead is among the figures depicted in the Water Street mural in Norwich.

MacLeish's research revealed that Mead was fourteen years old on March 1, 1776, when he enlisted in Norwich as a private in the company commanded by Captain John McGregor in Colonel John Durkee's regiment. At the end of his year of service, he was discharged in New York and returned to Norwich. Mead enlisted with Durkee and McGregor a second time. His name appears on muster rolls for Valley Forge from December 1777 to June 1778. While there, he became ill with smallpox and was hospitalized for two months. Mead's unit was discharged at Peekskill, New York. Early military records show Mead received solder's pay of $10.04 for his service in the Continental army in July 1783. He married and moved to Oneida, New York, where he raised sheep and spun and wove the wool. After a fire destroyed their home, he and his wife moved to Montrose, Iowa, with the Mormons, according to the biography on the town's website.

It seems clear that Mead was a valued member of the community. He had to appear in person at Fort Madison to collect his veteran's pension, and two local leaders accompanied him to speak about how highly he was esteemed in the community.

Cato Mead died around April 25, 1846, followed by his wife, who died ten days later. Mead is believed to be the only known Black Revolutionary War veteran buried west of the Mississippi River.

Job Primus/Amasel/Lathrop (1752–1822)

In 1752, an enslaved man named Primus Arms and his wife, Venus, had a son they named Job. They were enslaved by Ebenezer Lathrop of Norwich, and sometimes their surname was given as Lathrop, according to genealogist John Mills. Primus and Venus were sold to Ebenezer Lathrop's cousin Simon, but Job was kept with Ebenezer. When the war began, Job enlisted in the army, and records show his surname as Primus, Mills found.

According to *Black Roots in Southeastern Connecticut* (1980), authors Barbara W. Brown and James M. Rose found Job's May 9, 1756 baptismal record at First Church in Norwichtown. They quote Windham County pension records, which show him enlisted in Colonel John Durkee's regiment as Job Primus in March 1776; Captain Jedidiah Waterman was his commanding officer. He was discharged on January 1, 1777, at Trenton, New Jersey.

While still enslaved, Job and his wife, Sylvia, were married in 1774. Caleb Huntington paid sixty dollars to buy Job from his cousin Ebenezer and freed him on June 2, 1778, according to Windham land records. On October 25, 1779, Job used his army pay to purchase Sylvia for thirty dollars from David Ripley of Windham, authors Brown and Rose found.

After they were married, the couple used Amasel as their surname. Job and Sylvia had eight children: Job (1774), Katy (1778), Cyrus (1782), Primus (1783), Sylvia (1784), Lucinda (1786), Joseph (1790) and Rodman (1791). After Sylvia's death, Job married Keturah Williams on September 25, 1792, in Windham. Their children were Christopher (1793) and Alice (1794). By 1794, Job was able to buy land in Canterbury, Connecticut, where he lived with his family until his death on March 11, 1822.

Backus Fox

Another of the Norwich enslaved soldiers was Backus Fox, who was sold by Ezekiel Fox on June 27, 1777. The purchaser, Beriah Bill, then enlisted Fox in the Continental army, according to records held by Leffingwell House Museum. This was recorded in March 1781 with the City of Norwich, which is, thus far, the only information available.

BIBLIOGRAPHY

Books

Brown, Barbara W., and James M. Rose. *Black Roots in Southern New England 1650–1900*. Vol. 8 in the Gale Genealogy and Local History Series. Gale Research Company, 1980. Online at the Internet Archive, https://archive.org.

Carso, Brian F. *Gideon's Revolution*. Three Hills Press, 2023.

Caulkins, Frances Manwaring. *History of Norwich, Connecticut*. Published by the author, 1845 and 1860; republished by John Trumbull Press, 1989.

Gerlach, Larry R. *Connecticut Congressman: Samuel Huntington 1731–1796*. American Revolution Bicentennial Commission, 1976.

Goodrich, Charles A. *Character Sketch from Lives of the Signers of the Declaration of Independence*. 3rd ed. Thomas Mather, 1832. Available at the Library of Congress, https://www.loc.gov.

Huntington, Richard Thomas, Samuel Gladding Huntington and Samuel Huntington. *The Huntington Family in America: A Genealogical Memoir of the Known Descendants of Simon Huntington from 1633 to 1915*[…] Huntington Family Association, 1915. Online at the Internet Archive, https://archive.org.

Kelly, Jack. *God Save Benedict Arnold: The True Story of America's Most Hated Man*. St. Martin's Press, 2024.

King, David C. *Benedict Arnold: The Traitor Within*. New Lights Press, 2014.

Nafie, Joan. *To the Beat of a Drum*. Old Town Press, 1975.

O'Keefe, Marian, and Catherine Smith Doroshevich. *Norwich Historic Homes & Families.* Pequot Press, 1967.

Perkins, Mary E. *Old Houses of the Ancient Town of Norwich 1660–1800.* Press of the Bulletin Co., 1895.

Rugh, Dayne E. *John Durkee: The Forgotten Story of Connecticut's Bold Man from Bean Hill.* Keys to History, 2024.

Stark, Bruce P. *Connecticut Signer: William Williams.* American Revolution Bicentennial Commission of Connecticut, 1975.

Thompson, Marvin G. *Connecticut Entrepreneur: Christopher Leffingwell.* American Revolution Bicentennial Commission of Connecticut, 1979.

Van Doren, Carl. *Secret History of the American Revolution.* Augustus M. Kelley, originally published 1941, reissued 1973.

Wallace, Willard M. *Connecticut's Dark Star of the Revolution: General Benedict Arnold.* American Revolution Bicentennial Commission of Connecticut, 1978.

———. *Traitorous Hero: The Life and Fortunes of Benedict Arnold.* Harper & Brothers, 1954.

Online Resources

Ancestry. "North America, Family Histories, 1500–2000." https://www.ancestry.com.

Connecticut Sons of the American Revolution, General Israel Putnam Branch No. 4. "Col. John Durkee, Norwichtown's Forgotten Hero." *Scarlet Standard* Historical Series 6 (September 1998). www.sarconnecticut.org/the-scarlet-standard-no-6.

Dictionary of Canadian Biography. "Benedict Arnold." https://www.biographi.ca.

Duke University Archives and Manuscripts. Philip Turner papers. History of Medicine Collection (David M. Rubenstein Rare Book & Manuscript Library). https://archives.lib.duke.edu/catalog/turnerphilip.

George Washington's Mount Vernon. The Center for Digital History at the Washington Library. https://www.mountvernon.org/library/digitalhistory.

Governor Trumbull House & Wadsworth Stable. "Governor Jonathan Trumbull." https://www.govtrumbullhousedar.org.

Graves, Charles B. "Dr. Philip Turner of Norwich, Connecticut." *Annals of Medical History* 10, no. 1 (Spring 1928): 1–24. https://pmc.ncbi.nlm.nih.gov/articles/PMC7940004.

Griffith, William R., IV. "10 Facts: Benedict Arnold and Peggy Shippen." American Battlefield Trust, July 27, 2021, updated July 26, 2024. https://www.battlefields.org.

Hauptman, Laurence M. "From Boston's Streets to Bunker Hill: Southern New England Indians in the American Revolution." *American Indian* (Magazine of the Smithsonian's Museum of the American Indian) 20, no. 1 (Spring 2019). https://www.americanindianmagazine.org.

Leffingwell House Museum/Society of the Founders of Norwich website. https://www.leffingwellhousemuseum.org.

Library of Congress. "American Revolution and Its Era: Maps and Charts of North America and the West Indies, 1750 to 1789." https://www.loc.gov/collections/american-revolutionary-war-maps.

———. "Documents from the Continental Congress and the Constitutional Convention, 1774 to 1789." https://www.loc.gov/collections/continental-congress-and-constitutional-convention-from-1774-to-1789.

Mills, John. "The Lathrop Family." Alex Breanne Corporation. https://alexbreanne.org/research/lathrop-family.

Museum of Connecticut History. "Governor Jonathan Trumbull." https://museumofcthistory.org/2015/08/jonathan-trumbull.

National Park Service. "General Huntington." https://www.nps.gov.

———. "Samuel Ashbow Jr." From *Patriots of Color*, researched and prepared by George Quintal, 2004. https://www.nps.gov/people/samuel-ashbow-jr.htm.

Society of the Cincinnati in the State of Connecticut. "The Forgotten Regiment: Huntington's Heroes Emerge from the Mists of History." https://www.theconnecticutsociety.org/engagements/forgotten-regiment.

INDEX

ABOUT THE AUTHOR

Tricia Staley is a retired history teacher and school administrator. Prior to becoming an educator, she was a newspaper reporter, editor and advertising/public relations consultant. She majored in history at the University of Massachusetts/Amherst and holds a master's degree and a sixth-year certificate from Sacred Heart University. She also has completed certificate programs in genealogy and maritime history. Tricia has long been active in community affairs and currently serves as president of the Friends of Slater Museum.

Norwich in the Gilded Age: The Rose City's Millionaire's Triangle was published by The History Press in 2014. An illustrated lecture and popular walking tour are based on her research for that book. Her second book, *Norwich and the Civil War*, came out in 2015. Tricia was the 2022 recipient of the Connecticut Society of Genealogists' Tell Your Family Story award. She is currently working on a family history and several other writing projects.

She and her husband, Bob, live in Norwich with their dog, Rosie. They have two grown children and two grandchildren.

Visit us at
www.historypress.com